BISON
BOOKS

Leoti L. West

The Wide Northwest

*Historic Narrative of America's Wonder Land
as Seen by a Pioneer Teacher*

Leoti L. West

INTRODUCTION BY
Josephine Corliss Preston

INTRODUCTION TO THE BISON BOOKS EDITION BY
Brenda K. Jackson

UNIVERSITY OF NEBRASKA PRESS
LINCOLN AND LONDON

© 1927 by Leoti L. West
Introduction to the Bison Books Edition © 2005 by Brenda K.
Jackson
Manufactured in the United States of America

First Nebraska paperback printing: 2005

Library of Congress Cataloging-in-Publication Data
West, Leoti L., 1851–1933.
The wide Northwest: historic narrative of America's wonder land
as seen by a pioneer teacher / Leoti L. West; introduction by
Josephine Corliss Preston; introduction to the Bison Books edition
by Brenda K. Jackson.
p. cm.
Originally published: Spokane, Wash.: Shaw & Borden, 1927.
ISBN-13: 978-0-8032-9858-3 (pbk.: alk. paper)
ISBN-10: 0-8032-9858-7 (pbk.: alk. paper)
1. West, Leoti L., 1851–1933. 2. Frontier and pioneer life—
Northwest, Pacific. 3. Teachers—Northwest, Pacific—Biography.
I. Title.
LA2317.W4A3   2005
979.5—dc22   2005015326

This Bison Books edition follows the original in beginning chapter
1 on arabic page 9; no material has been omitted.

BRENDA K. JACKSON

Introduction to the Bison Books Edition

Leoti West found nothing particularly exceptional in her decision, in 1878, to leave her Iowa home and her position as principal of the English department at Bayless Business College in Dubuque, to travel across the country to the eastern Washington frontier. West had longed for the opportunity "to be west and grow up with the country" (14). A letter from the Reverend. S. E. Stearns in March of 1878, offering a teaching position at the new school in Colfax, Washington Territory, placed the young woman's goal to move west squarely within her reach. Leoti West spent little time, if any, weighing the pros and cons of such a drastic move, and in July 1878 she boarded the train at Cedar Rapids for the first leg of her journey to the frontier.

West likely considered her relocation unworthy of note for a number of reasons. Life experiences had forced her to mature quickly, to take full and sole responsibility for her actions and decisions, and to deal with the results and any roadblocks placed in her path. She was a no-nonsense and practical woman. Her three-thousand-mile journey was not about the relocation of a single woman to the frontier, but rather about a teacher bringing educational opportunities to the inhabitants of the West. And though she may not have seen it, West's goals, and the means by which she set out to achieve them, were, in fact, most exceptional.

The records of Colfax Academy—so named by its trustees in December 1881—reveal that the need for both a school and a church was under discussion among the Colfax citizenry and Rev. S. E. Stearns, acting missionary for the American Baptist Home Mission Society of New York, beginning as early as the summer of 1876. The collection of funds for the construction of a single building to serve both purposes began at that time, but conflict between settlers and the local Native American population delayed the start of construction for more than a year. It is unclear if Leoti West realized that the American West she yearned to experience was very much a frontier in the late 1870s, with armed conflict between white and Native American populations, though quieted, still a possibility. It is completely clear, however, that the Colfax community looked forward to West's arrival, and with the church/school structure finally completed in 1878, "arrangements were perfected whereby the management of the school was undertaken by Miss Leoti L. West of Dubuque Iowa and the school was opened on Sep. 11th 1878."[1]

By the time West migrated to Washington Territory, female teachers were no longer a novelty, either on the frontier or in the nation's urban and rural centers. In fact, by the late nineteenth century women made up the majority of educators teaching at the primary levels throughout the United States and its western territories. The post–Revolutionary War era of the late eighteenth century, with its emphasis on the importance of an educated citizenry, had brought about this transition. Leaders of the young nation promoted and strongly encouraged at least a rudimentary education for boys and girls as a means by which to produce the continuous supply of republican sons required to lead the nation into the foreseeable future. A tremendous number of teachers was required to accomplish this ambitious educational goal, and women were encouraged to enter the profession. Touted as "natural" educators for young children who would respond to the nurturing only women could provide, female teachers made economic sense as well, particularly to community leaders in frontier towns and villages who had only limited economic resources but were determined to hire their first teacher. Female teachers could be secured at much lower rates of pay than their male counterparts. Some publications of the day suggest that female teachers forced their way into the profession, "elbowing" men out of their way, but it is important to note that by the mid-nineteenth century men were leaving teaching of their own volition—in droves. Farming, industry, and newly created white-collar opportunities in business promised far greater financial returns than did teaching.

Over time a number of studies have been undertaken for the purpose of identifying—"labeling"—the women who personally took on the responsibility of educating America and, in particular, the inhabitants of the American frontier. These studies reveal that female teachers came from a multitude of backgrounds and locations around the United States. In contrast to Leoti West's story, however, most of these young women did not intend to make a career of teaching and planned to engage in the profession for only a few years. For those farmers' daughters who had grown weary of life on the farm, as well as for middle-class daughters seeking escape from the restraints of "home," teaching provided a respectable "interlude" and allowed women to experience some independence during the years between their own schooling and their eventual marriages. For women left to their own devices, as well as to those without other means of support, teaching provided an alternative to the humiliation of "spinsterhood" or residency in the homes of siblings or other family members.

Reformer Catharine Beecher, in establishing the Dubuque Female Institute in the late 1840s, argued that teaching provided "the road to honourable independence and extensive usefulness where [a woman] need not outstep the prescribed boundaries of feminine modesty."[2] Beecher later helped form both the Board of National Popular Education and the American Women's Education Association, institutions at which female students perfected their frontier teaching skills.

The curricula at these teaching institutions prepared women for the circumstances and conditions they expected to face in their frontier schoolrooms—conditions that their contemporaries in the East would characterize as strange and probably unacceptable. Frontier teachers learned various methods of class management, since it was likely that a single classroom would hold students that ranged dramatically in age and level of educational achievement. A history of the Colfax Academy, written at mid-twentieth century, reported that the enrollees in Leoti West's first class in September 1878 numbered "seventeen young people, who had about eighth grade requirements."[3] The student population in one Idaho frontier schoolhouse just across the territorial border further explains this "eighth grade" average, and reveals that the levels of education achieved by twenty students who began the 1878 term ranged from no education at all to a significant amount of schooling in eastern locations before their migrations to the West.[4]

A number of teachers who traveled to the frontier faced, or at least feared, discipline problems arising from the diverse collection of students who made up their classroom populations.

BISON BOOKS INTRODUCTION

In 1857 Mary Ellis worried "what shall I do with the big boys this winter," and in 1869, during her first teaching assignment, Alice Money Lawrence revealed in a letter to her sister, "I had to keep all my scholars but one in at recess today, and I had to whip one boy—the first punishment of that kind that has been necessary."[5] Discipline problems aside, frontier schools, and the women who taught in them, were enormously important to their communities, and classroom populations soared. As a Missouri schoolteacher reported in a letter home, "I commenced School Monday the 7th of May with sixteen scholars. At the end of the week I had twenty two & the next Monday I had twenty five & this week I have twenty-nine & they say that more are coming."[6] Leoti West enjoyed similar success in Washington Territory. In the first three months of her first term, West's class had grown from the original seventeen to more than fifty—and by term's end nearly one hundred pupils crowded into the small schoolroom. According to Colfax historians, "as long as Miss West was head of the Academy it prospered."[7]

Classroom management skills did not represent the only "unique" aspect of teaching on the frontier: academies provided their teachers-in-training with methods of dealing with shortages, particularly with shortages of books. A number of frontier teachers attempted to solve this problem by establishing rudimentary frontier libraries, and in a September 1850 letter from the pioneer settlement of Cassville, Missouri, Martha Rogers wrote, "I thought that I would like to have a few books for a sort of circulating Library to excite a desire & taste for reading."[8] Rogers's objective was to make books available to both the Cassville citizenry at large and to her students, which also seems to be the motivation behind the actions of Colfax Academy leaders thirty years later. The March 1883 meeting of the Colfax Academy trustees resulted in the creation of a committee to

"solicit subscriptions for a needed library and school apparatus."
Leoti West served on that committee."[9]

Among female frontier teachers, a few capitalized on the independence and opportunity the profession afforded them, and Leoti West holds a place of distinction in this group. Among the first American women to hold professional management positions were women such as Sarah Raymond Fitzwilliam, who began as a teacher on the Illinois frontier, served as principal of a Bloomington, Illinois, high school in the 1860s, and worked as Bloomington's city superintendent of schools until 1892. In addition, Fitzwilliam published a manual of instruction in 1877, which was used by teachers throughout Illinois for a number of years.[10] Following her teaching career, Mary Johnstone served as principal, then as county superintendent of schools, in 1880s Montana. It is reported that, with her sister in tow, Johnstone "traveled from school to school in a light buggy, drawn by one horse, over dangerous roads, boarding with ranch families along the way."[11] Leoti West followed the lead set by these professional women and, after serving as a member of the Washington Territorial Board of Education, she served as principal for a number of schools in eastern Washington, was a member of the Washington teachers' examination board, and was assistant to Washington's superintendent of public instruction, among others. Fitzwilliam, Johnstone, West, and the many others educated the frontier population but also legitimized the term "professional woman" and paved the way for others who desired public over private lives in the West.

Leoti West may not have considered herself, or her life experiences, as exceptional, but those who read and enjoy *The Wide Northwest* will certainly come away with a different opinion. The unmarried woman who, at just twenty-seven years of age, chose an unknown future on the Washington frontier over the comfortable familiarity of Iowa became an instrumental cog in the wheel of public education in Washington, during the territorial phase and after statehood in 1883. During her fifty-plus years of teaching in Washington, West is said to have "sent more than 5,000 graduates on their way," and her years as an administrator allowed her to have an impact on thousands more. Her reminiscences first appeared in the Spokane, Washington, *Spokesman-Review* as a series of over one hundred pioneer sketches, and were collected and published as *The Wide Northwest: Historic Narrative of America's Wonder Land as Seen by a Pioneer Teacher* in 1927. Thanks to the University of Nebraska Press, and to the insight of its Bison Books editor, Heather Lundine, Leoti West's story is once again available to those with an interest in the West and the exploits and experiences of its female pioneers. When Leoti West died on December 22, 1933, at the age of 83, the *Spokesman-Review* lauded her as a "Beloved Woman" and the "Inland Empire's Most Famous Teacher."[12] It was a sentiment held by the thousands whose lives she touched and the thousands who undoubtedly considered everything about Leoti L. West as exceptional.

NOTES

1. Colfax College Board of Trustees, *Minutes and Records of Colfax Baptist Academy and Colfax College*, Manuscripts, Archives, and Special Collections, Washington State University Libraries, Pullman WA, cage 1555, n.p.

2. Julie Roy Jeffrey, *Frontier Women* (New York: Hill and Wang, 1979), 90.

3. "The Colfax Academy: A Brief History," ca. 1950, Manuscripts,

BISON BOOKS INTRODUCTION

Archives, and Special Collections, Washington State University Libraries, Pullman WA, cage 1592, n.p.

4. Sandra L. Myres, *Western Women and the Frontier Experience, 1800–1915* (Albuquerque: University of New Mexico Press, 1982), 249.

5. Glenda Riley, *The Female Frontier: A Comparative View of Women on the Prairie and the Plains* (Lawrence: University of Kansas Press, 1988), 105.

6. Polly Welts Kaufman, *Women Teachers on the Frontier* (New Haven: Yale University Press, 1984), 183.

7. "Colfax Academy Brief History," n.p.

8. Kaufman, *Women Teachers*, 188.

9. Colfax Board of Trustees, *Minutes and Records*, July 8, 1882.

10. Riley, *Female Frontier*, 106.

11. Riley, *Female Frontier*, 124.

12. "Leoti L. West Dies Suddenly," *Spokesman-Review* (WA), December 23, 1933.

CONTENTS

❦ ❦

INTRODUCTION

Miss West's narrative depicting the facts and interesting human events of early life in Washington and relating to school growth in the Northwest, presents a most interesting account of the fascinating experiences of educational pioneers.

Miss West has made an enviable record of service, first, in an academy at Colfax and later as Principal of Baker School, Walla Walla, which was probably one of the first brick school buildings built in Washington Territory.

Her distinguished service as an educator in Territorial days brought her to the forefront and in 1882 she was appointed as a member of the Territorial Board of Education, which position she held for a number of years. Her work as Principal of Baker School in Walla Walla; her service as a member of the County Board of Education of Walla Walla County and her efforts to organize and strengthen the city schools of Walla Walla; the county schools of Walla Walla; and the Territorial and state system of schools of Washington, make her story of the life of educational pioneers, doubly significant.

As one of the teachers in Baker School while Miss West was Principal, I am pleased to write this introduction of a book to be read by the many pupils and friends who have known and appreciated a woman of sterling worth and high ideals. Many others may learn of her for the first time through the heart interest stories contained in the pages of this book.

May all young teachers who read these pages from the pen of this noble woman receive inspiration for their work and renewed courage for the tasks before them.

MRS. JOSEPHINE CORLISS PRESTON
Superintendent of Public Instruction, State of Washington
OLYMPIA, WASHINGTON

CHAPTER I

MY EARLY LIFE

It was Charles Dickens who made the hero of his most popular novel, and the one thought to be his own autobiography say: "The clock began to strike and I began to cry simultaneously." Now, this was not my experience for unlike David, I was born at 1:30 o'clock Tuesday morning, March 18, 1851. I have credible authority for this fact, and I am told also that it was a stormy morning. There is no record that I entered the world crying, in fact I was said to be a good baby, not at all in accord with the tumultuous character of my birth month, nor even yet of the old adage, "Child of Tuesday full of grace." I seem to have been a misfit in both respects.

My earliest recollection dates to a time when I had reached the mature age of two and a half years. I sat upon the huge stone hearth in front of the equally huge fireplace in my maternal grandmother's living

9

room, playing with some baby chicks born too late in the fall to be trusted with the mother hen. My cousin Anna, somewhat older, and I had been so engaged for what seemed to me to be a long time and I wanted to do something else but Anna was still interested and refused. In desperation, I picked up one of the chicks and wrung its neck. Anna cried out and grandmother appeared upon the scene. Even at this late day, I seem to feel myself lifted and turned over her knee, while, in imagination, I seem still to feel the sting of that slipper which was so effectively applied. This may be the reason why many years later I selected the rubber shoe as an instrument of condign punishment. At any rate it cured me of any desire to take life maliciously thereafter. It was punishment well administered.

I grew up and received what little education I possess in the schools of my native state, Iowa, with a single year at Mt. Carroll Seminary in Illinois. That school is now known as the Frances Shimar Academy and is connected with the Chicago University.

My parents were of southern ancestry, and on the West side distantly related to Benjamin West, the painter. When I was ten years old, my father entered the army and four years later gave his life for his country. We were not well off, and I was anxious for an education. When I heard that the good people of the state had provided schools for the education of the children of her fallen brave, I said: "I am going to that school." Although grandmother, who was intensely aristocratic in her ideas held up her hands in horror at the thought, I carried my point and in my fifteenth year entered the school at Cedar Falls. A second year I arranged to keep the books of the institution for my board while I attended a small business college in the town. I had early developed into an expert penman.

Just prior to my seventeenth birthday, I returned home and opened a small private school for children, mostly German, but after six weeks the interesting disease known as the itch broke out in the community and my school closed. However, in the fall of that year, I was invited to return to the Cedar Falls Soldiers' Orphans' home to keep the books, and at the same time take charge of a primary class. Thus began a teaching career which was to continue for more than half a century. It is not my purpose to enter into tiresome details of the work of the next three years, but it is interesting to note that I was first paid $12.50 a month with board and laundry, then $15.00 and, finally, $25.00 for my services.

But I was anxious to continue my studies and so secured a place as a student teacher at the Mt. Carroll Seminary. Here I taught three and three quarter hours each day and took from three to four studies, keeping up with my classes. In addition to this, I did considerable work along clerical lines for the principal of the school. It is needless to say that when the year closed I was pretty well worn out and declined to return, although invited to do so at increased compensation.

The following year, I taught the school in our home district, and in the spring was invited to return to the Orphans' home as bookkeeper and assistant to the Superintendent with a salary of $400.00 a year and a month's vacation in summer. This was a fine wage at that date, and I accepted, but within two weeks of the time of my return one of the teachers came down with the measles and died. This threw me back into the school room where I remained, doing the other work as a side issue until we closed the institution in June, 1876. The State had provided three homes for the orphan children of soldiers, but as the children of suitable age grew fewer in number the schools were closed and the work consolidated at Davenport, and it was made a general orphans' home. The property at Cedar Falls was a valuable one and the state decided to turn it into a normal college, or school as it was then called.

I returned to Dubuque and entered Bayless' business college and completed a course in bookkeeping. That fall I was invited to go to Osage, Iowa, and become acting-preceptress of the Seminary at that place. During the winter I spent in this school, Hamlin Garland, who has become noted as a writer of western stories, was a student. At the close of the winter term I resigned and returned home. Immediately thereafter, President Bayless offered me a position as principal of the English department in his school which I accepted and taught for a period of fifty-four weeks without a vacation. Then the "lure of the great west" became so great that I resigned a most excellent opportunity to make a name for myself and considerable money and migrated to Washington Territory, which has been my home since.

I have omitted many things which might have been interesting to my readers but as this is essentially a record of my western career it has seemed fitting that this sketch be made as brief as possible.

—Leoti L. West.

CHAPTER II

MIGRATION TO WASHINGTON TERRITORY

Was it Shakespeare who said: "There is a divinity which shapes our ends, rough hew them how we may." No truer words were ever uttered. They are verified again and again in the lives of men and women. Now, I do not propose to moralize, but I simply want to call attention to what is, to me, a most interesting fact. Just as my mind was turning to the Pacific coast as a place where I could carry on my work to good advantage an opening was being provided where I could come in touch with the young in a helpful way.

In May, 1877, I had accepted a position as principal of the English department in Bayless' Business College, at Dubuque, Iowa, but I wanted "to go west and grow up with the country." I needed physical growth, as I only weighed 186 pounds.

In the early fall of that year I wrote to a friend in California, asking him if he could locate me in a community where I could open a business college of my own. I was an expert penman and had a good knowledge of double entry bookkeeping. He replied that he knew of no opening in his state, but he had sent my letter to the Rev. J. C. Baker, superintendent of missions for Oregon and Washington, where there were many openings such as I desired.

Hearing nothing further, I had practically forgotten the matter when in March, 1878, I had a letter from the Rev. S. E. Stearns, written at Colfax, saying my letter had been sent to him by Mr. Baker, and adding further that the people of Colfax had just erected a small frame building to be used for school and religious purposes until such time as a suitable school building could be provided; that there was a large number of young people in the community growing up without adequate provision for their education; that the parents were not financially able to send these young people long distances to school; that he had showed my letter to the business men of the town, and they were unanimous in saying: "If she wrote that letter she is the teacher we want."

After considerable correspondence with Mr. Stearns and others and securing a written guarantee for my support the first year, I resigned my position, against the earnest protest of President Bayless, who said: "If you go out to the 'wild and woolly west' you will be scalped by the Indians or some other calamity will befall you."

But I persisted and made my plans to leave for

Washington territory as soon as possible. I want to say right here that I have never regretted the step.

It is interesting to note that President Bayless so far overcame his fear of the Indians as to allow his only son to cross, at a later date, the great divide and come to "sunny old Spokane," where he now resides.

On a delightful July evening I bade goodbye to friends and relatives and took a night train for Cedar Rapids, where I spent a delightful day with old-time friends. Another night ride and I was in Council Bluffs, where I met Miss Flora E. Stough, a young music teacher, who had decided to go west with me, as there was need of her services in Colfax.

We were soon across the Missouri and on board the Union Pacific train bound for San Francisco. The train equipment would be considered meager today, but we had a comfortable car and while we lacked the privacy of the present day Pullman, each passenger was allowed two seats, and I found one could sleep comfortably that way.

The day's ride through Nebraska was interesting, but monotonous. One soon tires of the almost flat surface of the Platte River Valley, but the countless prairie dog villages which lined the railroad on either side were a source of amusement to us all. There the little creatures sat upon their haunches "on dress parade," it would seem, for our special benefit. Late in the afternoon we saw in the distance the foothills of the mountains and the next morning we reached Cheyenne, then as now a most interesting city.

Here we spent several hours waiting for a delayed train from Kansas City and just before we started a young man who, with a party of other gentlemen, was en route for Elko, Nev., boarded the train. This young man, now the most famous man in the world in his line of human endeavor, was none other than Thomas Edison. He did not, at this time, give any very marked evidence of the greatness that was later to come to him.

Another man also came aboard and found a seat in our car who was to prove an inspiration to me. This was Professor Collier, a naturalist from the Oregon state university.

The professor had been out on research work for his school and was well up in the flora, fauna and geological formation of the country through which we were passing. I found him an instructive and agreeable companion. He proved especially helpful in giving me the correct pronunciation of Pacific coast proper names of which I was woefully ignorant. Hardly a stop but he was out of the car only to return with some curious flower or stone about which he was able to give me much valuable information.

Just prior to reaching Oakland, Calif., three children boarded the train who had gone to school to me two years before in Iowa, bearing a message from their mother, a widow, that she wanted to entertain me for a few days. This I consented to and then went north into Mendocino county to see a sister and two brothers who were employed in the redwoods of that county at a place called Little River, now Willetts, then to Ukiah, where I spent the night with a cousin.

This cousin was a practical joker, as I later found to my discomfort. He said: "Now, you are likely to be ill when you go aboard the ship, but if you will take a good dose of this medicine which I am giving you, you will find it helpful." I thanked him and placed the bottle in my bag.

Two days later we boarded the steamship George W. Elder, then the finest ship on the line to Portland. We were assigned a stateroom on the upper deck which we visited to find another woman in the upper berth ill with the ague. Disposing of our belongings, we went on deck to watch the ship as she passed through the Golden Gate. Just as we passed out, the dinner bell rang and we went into the dining room to find a wonderful feast spread out for our refreshment.

I have always felt that the ship's officials know that the combined odors of so many kinds of food were more than likely to make one ill, and so they act accordingly in order to reduce the board bill. I had eaten but a few mouthfuls when I felt decidedly squeamish and so rushed on deck. Proceeding to my stateroom, I took a good dose of the medicine (whisky) and you may imagine the rest. For a time it seemed as if I should be turned inside out. Then it was that I experienced that peculiar form of illness which Mark Twain has called the "Ohmy." However, I crawled into my berth and after an hour or so felt more comfortable.

I remained quietly in bed until the next morning and then about nine o'clock ordered a light breakfast and about 10 went on deck feeling entirely fit. Near noon I went into the cabin and sat down near the stairway coming up from the dining room. Mr. Fox, a Jewish gentleman from Oregon City, sat near me and after a little he said:

"Do you occupy No. 43?" When I responded in the affirmative, he said: "I really feel as though you had saved my life. I was lying in my berth next door desperately sick and had about made up my mind to jump overboard and so put an end to my misery, but I heard you folks in your room having such a good time that I thought 'What a fool I am'; I arose, dressed and went out on deck and have been feeling fine ever since."

Just at this point a large and fine looking gentleman came staggering up the stairway, so sick he could hardly stand. As he turned the corner, the ship lurched, he lost his balance and sat down on my lap. The poor fellow stammered:

"Excuse me," and I responded: "Certainly, I am not accustomed to holding gentlemen in this way but under the circumstances you are excusable. Later in the day he returned, made suitable apology and we became good friends.

During the day, I found that Professor Collier was on board, he had been detained longer than he expected and was now on his way home. Through him, I was introduced to a most delightful lady, a Mrs. Finney, the widow of the celebrated evangelist of that name. She was en route to visit relatives at Pilot Rock, Ore.

The rest of the voyage was accomplished without mishap of any kind and we reached Portland on Wednesday morning just after the boat had left for her trip up the river. We were elected to spend two days in the city. Portland was at this time the wealthiest city of its size in America, and a really beautiful place.

Early Friday morning we boarded a fine river steamer which carried us to a point about where the town of Bonneville is now located. Here we took a narrow gauge railroad for several miles, then another steamer to The Dalles, another railroad for a short distance, and then a third boat which took us to Wallula where we were to leave the river.

We spent the night on the last boat and arrived in Wallula in the early forenoon. After a wait of some four hours we went aboard the Dr. Baker railroad, running into Walla Walla, 30 miles away. The coach was a cattle car with boards running lengthwise of the car for seats. After more than three hours of riding through sagebrush and sand, we reached our objective only to find the hotels and boarding houses all full to overflowing.

Here we had to wait until Monday for a stage to Colfax. Fortunately I had letters of introduction to the Adams brothers, merchants of Walla Walla, and after presenting them we were well cared for during our two days' stay in this town, which was destined to be my home at a later date. Walla Walla at this time had a population of about 2,000, although the city claimed many more than that.

On Monday noon we boarded a large Concord stage coach for Dayton en route for Colfax. The day was hot, the dust terrible, and a drunken man kept things lively for a while. He finally went to sleep and snored for our benefit until we reached Dayton, then a fine little town. Here we left the stage and were to be carried the rest of the way by buckboard, a vehicle new to me. We arrived in Dayton about 5 o'clock and were to remain until 10 before we could proceed. I was warm and dusty and suggested to Miss Stough that we secure a room and clean up a little before we had dinner. We were ushered into a room containing two beds and after we had washed and rearranged our hair and clothing we felt much better.

While at dinner, which was a good one, I suggested that we pay our bill before going back upstairs and then we should be ready for the stage when it came. When I stepped to the counter and asked Mr. Gorman, the landlord, for our bill, he said: "Two dollars please." But I called attention to a sign overhead which said, "Meals 50 cents. beds 50 cents," and when I said: "We didn't use the beds, but are perfectly willing to pay a reasonable price for the soiled towels, etc. He told us we must pay full price for the rooms anyway. We gave him the $2, and then I went up to the room, washed as many times as there were clean towels, and disarranged the beds so that they would have to be made again before they could be used.

I then went to the parlor to wait, feeling that I had gotten something for my money anyway. Here I found a woman in a towering rage. She, too, had been given a room for herself and husband for which they had been charged $2, and while I was getting my money's worth, they were ordered out of the room that it might be given to another guest for the night.

At 10 o'clock we were crowded into the two-seated buckboard, the mail under our feet. Mr. C. G. Linington, a burly man going into Colfax to start a private bank, his wife, and William Jones, who afterwards became wealthy and died in Tacoma a couple of years ago, were on the back seat, while Miss Stough, the driver and myself were in front. Mr. Parker, the driver, must have weighed at least 225 pounds, so you can imagine we were well packed in.

Our four horses had given place to two, but they were good travelers and we made fine time. At Pataha City, about three miles from Pomeroy, which did not exist at that time, we were due for breakfast and to change horses. It was a bright moonlight night and I amused myself by turning sideways every little while to watch Mr. Jones. He had been to a party the night before and so found it hard to keep awake. Part of the time his head rested on Mrs. Linington's shoulder and then with a sudden start, it was switched to close proximity with a wheel of the vehicle.

That breakfast I shall never forget. We had fried chicken, but the one who dressed the fowl forgot to divest it of anything except the larger feathers and we had to skin it before eating. At 6 a. m. we are on the road again and crossed the Snake River at Pennawawa, about the middle of the forenoon.

As we left the ferry Mr. Jones asked the driver to stop while he alighted in order to purchase a water melon as a treat to the party. The melon was fine and when we had eaten it Mr. Jones' face presented a most grotesque appearance. The streaks of dust and watermelon juice alternated until he had a countenance which would have done credit to a clown.

We climbed the long Pennawawa hill, and some time in the afternoon the driver halted and said: "There is Colfax."

In the meantime, however, I had been quizzing him about the town, and among other things I asked if he knew Theophilus Smith, saying that I had received a number of urgent letters from him and so supposed he had a large family to educate. Mr. Parker laughed and said:

"Yes, I know Sirup Smith, but he is an old bachelor. He has a greenhouse two miles from town and when he isn't busy there he hauls freight from Walla Walla for John C. Davenport, the principal merchant of the town."

Then he told us how he had earned the name Sirup. One night as he was returning with a load of freight for the store he camped on Snake River. A man camping near by had a dog which Mr. Smith coveted. After some conversation, the man traded the dog for a keg of sirup. Of course, Mr. Smith had to make it good with the store, but the name clung to him always thereafter.

But to return to Colfax as it appeared to our interested view. Imagine a long narrow valley several hundred feet wide, with a sluggish stream flowing through it, while on either side were two high hills, almost perpendicular; a lot of plain board houses, a two-story frame building with mansard roof, the Ewart house, and the little church building where I was to teach for about five years, and you have Colfax.

My journey, which took nearly two weeks of time and cost more than $200, was at an end. I had become a citizen of Eastern Washington, where I shall likely spend the remainder of my life.

CHAPTER III

BEGINNING COLFAX ACADEMY, 1878

When we drove to the entrance of the Ewart house on August 20 we found a number of the townspeople waiting to catch a glimpse of the imported teacher who had been expected for several days. Captain Ewart, the landlord, and his good wife met me at the door and gave me a cordial welcome. As long as they lived, I looked upon them as my kind friends.

Early the next morning I went to the office to see about my baggage, and Robert Bruce, the clerk, asked me to write the bill of fare for the day. While I was writing Captain Ewart came in, and as we stood talking some one entered and said:

"Sirup Smith is coming."

Almost at once there stood in the door a tall, stoop-shouldered man, thin, angular and with a straggling beard streaked with gray. A semi-benevolent smile everspread his countenance. He came forward and was introduced. We talked for a little while about my trip and the work I had come to take up. Then, after handing me the key to the school building, he took his leave.

Now, I am a good deal of a physiognomist and I was interested to study his face and general personality. As I noticed the way the upper lips pressed down over his teeth and the lines about his eyes and mouth I thought:

"Here is a good man, but he is narrow in his views of life, and most intolerant of the actions of others. He is set in his ways and hard to convince that he might be wrong. Future acquaintance with the man proved that I was entirely right in my conclusions.

Soon after his departure, I walked one block to the schoolhouse and entered, being anxious to become familiar with my future surroundings. Imagine a small frame bulding 26 feet by 50 feet with a narrow entry 8 feet by 26 feet, from which two doors led into the main room, or should I say auditorium?

The room was 12 feet high and Wainscoted to a height of three feet. There were 28 homemade double desks in the room, half on each side, snug against the wall. Ten long benches graced the center. These benches had a single six-inch board as a back, properly braced.

Just between the two doors was a large stove with a horizontal pipe, running nearly the entire length of the room and entering a flue in the extreme rear of the building. On this end of the room there **was a** narrow raised platform upon which were placed a teacher's table with a single drawer, two raw-hide bottomed chairs and a small organ.

The ceiling had been given a single coat of white paint, and the walls above the wainscot was clothed. There were three windows on either side of the room and in lieu of lamps, small cleats containing an auger hole had been placed on the window jams. In the event of an evening service, candles were placed in these holes. You can imagine the brilliant illumination thus afforded.

Lack of space will prevent my introducing to you personally many of the good people of the community who were specially helpful to me in my undertaking. I shall simply call attention to them as I continue these chronicles. I just want to say, however, that no finer or more hospitable class of people ever lived upon the face of the earth than these same Palousers. They were as the "salt of the earth." But there is one man and a journey of which I must speak at this time.

Early in the week, following my coming, the Rev. S. E. Stearns arrived and came to the hotel to meet me. I was informed that he had planned a trip which he thought I ought to take before I began immediate preparations for the opening of school. He further announced that he should be glad to use his buck-board in conveying me to the people he wanted me to see.

Father Stearns, as nearly every one called him, was an elderly man, not careful in his attire. He was of medium size with bushy brown beard, now almost gray. He had a kindly countenance and you knew at once he was a friend you could tie to. He always made me think of John the Baptist as I have visualized that noted Bible character.

Early in the afternoon we left Colfax and drove to the residence of L. T. Bragg, auditor of Whitman County for many years, one of the finest men in the country. Mr. Bragg had taken a homestead in a draw just off Rebel flat. Here he lived with his family, consisting of a wife, three children and a hired man. John Chestnut by name. I mention the last named particularly because he purchased Mr. Bragg's farm at a later date and married Emma Felch, one of my girls. Still later, their eldest daughter, Mabel, married my nephew, Dr. Mell A. West. They with their family now live in the town of Cheney, where Mell practices medicine. The house was comfortable and the Braggs were hospitality personified.

After supper (notice how primitive we were) Father Stearns said:

"I have made an appointment to preach at the schoolhouse on the flat."

We all walked the short distance to the school building which was a small affair. In a short time, Nora Odell and Effie Ringer, nieces of Mrs. Bragg, arrived, and soon thereafter, the Felch family, who lived on the other side of the flat.

COLFAX ACADEMY

There were no lights and so Mr. Felch, who, by the way, was an ardent Methodist, went back to his home and in a few minutes returned with a single candle and the fashionable candlestick. This was placed on the stove and Mr. Stearns preached his sermon. I do not remember what he said, except the text which was: "And God said, 'Let there be light,' and there was light."

The next morning, we rode on down the flat to the home of old Grandpa Owen, a dear old gentleman from Missouri. Here he lived to be near his six daughters, all of whom were married and, at this time, lived not far away. After grandpa had killed a couple of chickens in honor of our coming, he took his buggy and started to round up several of his daughters to meet the new teacher.

This time the chickens were properly prepared and we found that grandma, despite her age, was an excellent cook.

May I here digress to relate a little story about this same dear old lady. She had a cow for sale. A certain man came to see the cow. After looking her over he asked:

"And what do you want for her?"

Grandma naively answered:

"I want thirty dollars but I would take twenty-five."

You can guess what she received for her cow.

One of the daughters present, Mrs. George J.

Buys, later removed to Walla Walla and I was privileged to board with her just as long as a certain Bible character served his father-in-law for a wife and then didn't get the one he wanted the first time. Can you guess who he was and how long he served?

The next morning we started for the home of Father Stearns, on Four Mile, about half way between Palouse and Moscow, Idaho. Here, on either side of a narrow canyon running down to the creek, he had taken for himself a homestead where his sister and her husband kept house for him, the Brother-in-law, Mr. Williams, doing what little work was done on the ranch. This pioneer home was a real home, but meager, indeed, in its appointments. It was here I was introduced to the immense cabbages, carrots and other vegetable products produced in the Palouse country.

On Sunday we listened to Mr. Stearns preach at Moscow, but not from the same text. The first of the week I was back in Colfax, preparing for the opening of school in which everybody took a vital interest.

It was September 11, 1878, that I opened school with 17 young people, not small children, but pupils of about eighth grade requirements at the present time. Then they averaged much older than now. The school grew rapidly until by Christmas I had more than 50 enrolled and before the end of the year, in June, nearly 100.

COLFAX ACADEMY

No matter what the occupation of the man, every citizen in Colfax and vicinity was my friend and vied with each other in helping me out with my work, whether they had children or not. Indeed, some of my staunchest friends were men without family ties who wanted to see me "put it over," as we express it today.

For the first year I did practically all the teaching myself, with a little help from some of the older girls in hearing a recitation now and then. We were greatly handicapped in having no suitable place for a recitation room. The entry was often too cold and, besides, was not a good place to send the pupils.

However, in spite of all our difficulties, we closed the school and I had made my guarantee for the first year. From that on I was thrown upon my own resources.

At the present time our school district comprise a limited stretch of territory. It was different in pioneer days. My district began on the south with the Snake River. It extended on the west to the Cascades, on the east to the Rockies and on the north to the north pole.

Like the old-time Methodist preacher, I had a hard time covering it all, but I made the attempt any way. It was only lack of boarding places that prevented the school from growing far beyond my ability to care for those who desired to come.

But there are some outstanding incidents connected

with this first year's work which I must narrate. It was soon apparent that the long horizontal stove pipe was a failure. When I wanted it changed by placing the stove near the center of the room, Mr. Smith said:

"No, it can not be done. The stove must stay where it is."

However, there was a meeting of the church about that time and I presented my request and was instructed to have the stove placed where I wanted it. Poor Mr. Smith found I could be just as determined as he.

Again, it was not long until the clothed walls became dingy from smoke and dust and I wanted them papered, and again I had run up against a snag. Mr. Smith said "No."

There was to be no church meeting for several weeks and I was much depressed. When I went to my dinner I felt and looked blue. I found Mr. and Mrs. W. H. Davenport, Leon Kuhn and Julius Lippitt, business men of the town, at the table. We always ate our meals together at this time.

When I made known my grievance they, of course, expressed sympathy. A little later, after I had gone to the parlor, Mr. Kuhn came up and said:

"Well, sis, go ahead and have the church papered and Julius and I will foot the bill." Again Sirup failed in having his way.

The good people to whom I have alluded, together

with myself, made a family of five. We called the young married people "Pa" and "Ma." Leon was my older brother and Julius and I were twins, there being just a month's difference in our ages.

I want to say here and now that these two Jewish gentlemen were as good friends as I ever had. I hold them in grateful remembrance.

Mr. Kuhn passed away several years ago and Mr. Lippitt is now a resident of Portland, Ore., almost blind. He has, I think, an interest in the Old National Bank of this city. The Davenports now live in Spokane.

We needed lamps for the church to replace the cleats which had been in use. One Saturday morning I wrote on a slip of paper Mr. Stearns' text, "Let there be light." In company with Mrs. Davenport, I started out. The first house next the hotel was a saloon kept by a Mr. Johnson. He stood in the door. I told him what I wanted and he said:

"Come into my office. I will give you something."

I went in. He handed me $3 from the till and asked if I would have a drink, which I declined. In less than two hours we had visited all the places of business, including three saloons and two places where they made beer, and we had money enough to go to the store and order the lights needed put in the church for the Sunday service next day. So there was light without a name being written on my subscription list.

As the Christmas season approached, preparations were made for a big tree upon which there should be presents for everybody. My school building was just a block from Davenport's store, and I had difficulty in keeping the pupils away from the store at recess time. I announced that any who were tardy in future would be locked out until noon.

Six of the girls—Mamie James, Dora Lansdale, Mary Kennedy, Josie Davenport, Mary Bowman and Nettie Ewart—had arranged to meet Mrs. Ewart that particular morning at the store to help them select a Christmas present for me. They decided to risk it anyway, and when they returned the door was locked and they had to go home until noon.

At first, they were inclined to give the beautiful vases they had purchased to some one else. Later they thought better of it, as it would be a splendid way "to heap coals of fire on my head." The coals were not hot enough to burn, however.

Among the many presents I received was an autograph album, which was just then becoming popular. When I asked Mr. Kuhn and Mr. Livingstone to write their names sometime later, Mr. Kuhn wrote a German sentiment which I could not read and Mr. Livingstone scrawled this delightful sentiment.

"Fair angel of earth

Bless the hour that gave thee birth—

Sweet as flowers in the morn."

COLFAX ACADEMY

It was such an utterly inappropriate sentiment when applied to me that I have kept it all these years as a curio.

One of our chief sources of amusement during the cold days of winter was skating. Practically everybody skated. Just two incidents:

One afternoon I started to go round the pond with Link Davenport holding one hand and Eugene Rice the other. Everything went well until my skate struck a snag and down I went on my back. The boys insisted I cracked the ice, while the gallant young gentlemen sped away for safety!

Again, Nettie Ewart and Mamie James were teaching Dick Wright to skate. They were holding his hands and doing well, but I skated up behind and put my hands on his shoulders. Everything went well for a time, but by some mischance he fell, sending the girls to right and left while I went straight over his head and landed on the ice some distance ahead.

At the close of the school year, and after an outing which I shall describe in the next article, I secured a pony (cayuse) and began scouring the Palouse hills for pupils. This I did each of the four summers I spent in Colfax.

Did you ever know a child who until the fifth year of his age was strong and husky and then because of overindulgence of fond parents he became sickly and inert and finally filled a premature grave? This is exactly what happened to the Colfax academy.

THE WIDE NORTHWEST

Its foster parents (all good people, and I have not a word to say against them) had a vision as to the wonderful things a college might accomplish in some distant future. The child was pampered, the infant, just out of swaddling clothes, changed his name. Large sums of money were raised and squandered on him. He lingered for some years and finally died, "Peace be to his ashes."

The last year of my connection with the school I enrolled 90 young men and women, not including a dozen children in the primary. Surely a fine beginning for a young school in a new country! The reason I was able to do this was because, no matter what a man's business, he was my friend.

I knew no social classes so far as the school was concerned. Indeed, I should have starved to death had I drawn the lines too closely. The saloon men and the gamblers were among my staunch friends. They sent their children to school and paid the tuition promptly. I shall never cease to regard these men and women as among the finest I have ever known. When taken as a whole they compared more than favorably with the vast multitude I have come in touch with during my career as a teacher of youth.

CHAPTER IV

A SUMMER OUTING

Of all the beautiful pictures which hang in Memory's
   hall,

The scenes of dear old Colfax, they seem the best
   of all.

The paraphrase of lines by Alice Carey illustrates
fully how I regard my work in Colfax. It was here
that I came in touch with young people in a way
vitally essential to their future well being. They were
so shut out from the centers of civilization and their
parents were unable financially to send them long distances to attend school where they might acquire
that secular knowledge so necessary to fit them successfully to cope with the realities of life.

One of the old-time residents said in my hearing
recently:

"No one ever came to Colfax whose coming was

looked forward to with greater interest than that which attended the coming of Miss West."

This, coupled with the fact that I made good, is compensation for years of toil and privation, for I experienced both.

Do not understand me to say that I cared more for these young people than I did for those in other localities where I taught. They are all alike dear to me. It was only that the need was so much greater here and there were plenty of teachers in the other places who were anxious for my position and who might have been even more successful than I.

In Colfax I was "the" teacher. Time and again I have had these boys and girls come to me and say:

"I don't know what we would have done without you at this critical period of our lives."

Some of them who have been most successful in business have said that it was I who gave them the training for their work. In an article to follow I shall make you acquainted with some of them, not "my pets," but those of whom, like a fond mother, I am proud.

They have made and are making good in their particular lines of human endeavor. Surely this is compensation enough and I am amply rewarded, although I went to Colfax with $500 in cash, gave nearly five years of my life and left there $50 in debt.

How different from C. G. Linington, who went in

A SUMMER OUTING

on the same buckboard with me, with $8,000, and in less than two years went out with $17,000!

But my readers will think me like the preacher who announces his text and then forgets all about it until the conclusion of his sermon.

"Would you be willing to make one of a party of people who plan to go on a camping trip in the near future? Uncle Jake Miller, the veteran stage driver of Eastern Washington, is in town and has consented to go, but he stipulates that this is on condition that you go with him as his guest."

So spoke one of the residents of Colfax, then the metropolis of the Inland Empire, with its 300 people. This was before Spokane Falls began to put on greatness.

How could I do other than accept, when this invitation came from a man of whom I had never heard prior to this time? Our plans were soon completed and one afternoon early in July, 1879, we were ready to start. A few words as to the personnel of the party. There were Captain Ewart, his wife and three daughters, Frankie, Nettie and Ada. By common consent, the captain was chosen commander of the expedition. He was from Missouri, had been a merchant and a farmer and was now mine host of the hotel.

John C. Davenport, his wife and two daughters, Josie and Eva, and his son Link. Mr. D. was easily the leading man in the community at this time. He

39

was an astute business man, honest and dependable in every way, but venturesome in his deals. He made fortunes easily and lost them just as easily. Josie later became the wife of C. B. Hopkins, editor of telephone fame, and later United States marshal for western Washington. I could tell a secret of how a certain book in her desk in my schoolroom was the hiding place of letters which passed between them, but I forbear.

Judge E. N. Sweet, his delightful wife and daughter, Edna. The judge was receiver of the U. S. land office, a dignified gentleman, who had always a cigar between his lips.

C. B. King, owner of the stage line from Colfax to Spokane Falls. He later, in connection with James Monaghan, founded the town of Coeur d'Alene, Idaho; was also one of the founders of the Traders' National bank of Spokane Falls, and still later owned a 1600-acre farm at Hayden Lake, where he built a magnificent home.

Leon Kuhn, hardware merchant; Julius Lippitt, general merchandise; Miss Flora Stough, J. B. Upton, Dr. P. D. Bunnell and wife, Uncle Jake Miller and the writer. There were some others who joined the party at a later date.

We dispatched a freight wagon about noon, and at 1 p. m. we were on our way. Most of the party rode in two-seated hacks, but Uncle Jake and I brought up the rear with our really "nobby rig." The road

out of Colfax at that time to the north was a steep
grade several miles in length. When the top was
reached, Uncle Jake stopped his horses and said:

"Miss West, I hope you'll excuse me, but I must
have a drink. I have used it for so long that I can
not do without it for any length of time." He handed
me the reins and took from a receptacle in the rear
of the buggy a large bottle, which he politely passed
over to me. When I declined with thanks, he took
for himself a liberal quantity and we drove on.

The day was superb and the roads excellent for
that period, when paved roads were unheard of.
Rather early in the afternoon, we arrived at the city
of Farmington, then almost as large as at the present
time, where we spent an hour or more. Uncle Jake
visited the chief store of the town and came back with
a big bag of candy for me and a large bottle of Florida
water, which the girls of the party found most ac-
ceptable while it lasted. After leaving Farmington,
we drove on for several miles, then stopped for supper
and the night.

It was so warm and delightful that we decided not
to pitch our tents but to sleep in the open. However,
several of the wagons were driven near a rail fence
and some of us made beds upon the ground, throwing
a tent from the hack to the fence as a protection from
the dew. This was a wise precaution as we had a
heavy dew that night, and the beds without this cover
were moist in the morning.

THE WIDE NORTHWEST

I shall never forget that night. We sat by a camp fire, sang, joked, told stories, and had a good time generally until late. Then when we went to bed I found myself with several girls under one of the wagon covers and next the hack wheel on one side and with Frankie Ewart on the other vainly trying to find a comfortable spot. She finally crawled over on me and neither pinches nor persuasive words would dislodge her, she calmly remarking that she had found a soft spot and proposed to stay by it. I have never since been able to decide whether she referred to my avoirdupois or to my disposition, but I am inclined to the latter view.

After an early breakfast, we drove some miles until we reached the California ranch and here we made camp while Mr. King took Uncle Jake's buggy and made a pilgrimage to the residence of Major Wimpy on Hangman Creek (euphonious name) after the daughter, Miss Belle, who was ere many months to become Mrs. King. The winter previous, Belle had gone to school to me. This is the only instance during my long career as a teacher when I had a mother and son in school at the same time, for Homer King was a student in the academy at that time.

I am not quite clear as to where we spent the second night out but before noon of the third day, we reached Coeur d'Alene lake and here Colonel Merriam, commander of the post, met us and invited us to make camp inside the military reservation. This was an unusual honor, and was duly appreciated.

A SUMMER OUTING

The soldiers were detailed to help us pitch our tents. They brought hay for beds and we were soon nicely located right on the banks of the beautiful lake. Added to this, we were furnished a number of boats which proved to be a great source of enjoyment. In my anxiety to show the folks that I had not forgotten my early training in that line on the Father of Waters," I rowed a boat 11 miles that first day. As a result, both hands were blistered clear across and I had worn out two pairs of gloves. A dance, a lake party in the moonlight, rides and sundry other diversions made the four days of our stay here all too short.

Leaving Coeur d'Alene, we drove down the beautiful Spokane Valley toward Spokane Falls of which we had heard much. In all the distance of more than 30 miles, there was just one house, used as a store and dwelling. That was at Spokane Bridge. I remember we talked much of the beauty of our surroundings and expressed regret that this could never become the home of many people because of the rocky character of the soil. Now this same section has been made to "rejoice and blossom as the rose." How little one can judge of the future by the present.!

When we arrived at the Little Spokane Falls, we stopped for several hours for lunch and to watch the turbulent water as, tumbling and roaring, it made its way through the narrow defile in the rock which had been worn away for it in past ages. We now call this point Post Falls.

When we had arrived at a point on the river some 10 miles from the town of Spokane Falls, we stopped for supper and the night. It was found that we had no bread, and it fell to my lot to make a supply of "the staff of life" for the company.

Imagine an immense dish pan, a quantity of flour, baking powder, lard, river water and an extra liberal supply of dust and sand and you have the ingredients of that bread which, when baked by the men in frying pans before the camp fire, was pronounced by many as the best bread they ever ate. On a camping trip, one can not be too fastidious.

The next morning, we had our first glimpse of Spokane Falls. Here we were invited by Father Havermale, the old-time Methodist minister of the section, to make camp in his yard near where the Great Northern depot is now located. At this place, we were joined by W. H. Davenport and wife, F. J. Wolfendon and others.

Several pleasant days were spent here. We drank in the grandeur of the marvelous falls and the superlative beauty of our surroundings to our hearts' content. Including Mr. Cannon and Mr. Glover, there were approximately 75 people here at the time.

I never cross the Monroe street bridge in these later days without the feeling that it was little less than sacrilege to sacrifice so largely the glorious falls for purposes of commercial gain. The inevitable dance and other amusements were provided for us but we were finally obliged to move onward.

A SUMMER OUTING

The next stop was at Medical Lake, where we bathed in its waters and were assured that it was a sure cure for certain forms of disease, notably rheumatism. A couple of days here and Uncle Jake and Mr. King left us to see some settler with whom Mr. K. had business. When we reached the point where they were to again join our party, we found Uncle Jake prone upon the ground, suffering from several bruises and a general shaking up. The horses had taken fright, run away and both the men had been thrown from the buggy. Neither the conveyance nor Mr. K. had been injured.

When I went to Uncle Jake and asked if there was anything I could do for him he said:

"I don't suppose you would give a fellow a drink of whisky?"

I thought otherwise and he soon had his drink. Like the kiss of a fond mother this acted as a panacea for his hurts and he was soon able to travel.

On the way home we passed through the site of Cheney, then a woodland; Spangle, a good-sized town, larger than Spokane; Rosalia, where there was a store and stage station; Cashup Davis', a store, a dance hall and a farm residence used for hotel purposes, and then home, all voting the trip a most enjoyable one, as well as educational in many senses of the word.

I not only saw the wonderful country to which I had come, but I learned more about human nature when placed under certain conditions than I had learned in all the years of my existence, prior to that time. I forbear explanations. Just take such a trip and you will learn them for yourselves.

May I say in conclusion that I have been over the route traveled a number of times since and have marveled at the wonderful growth and development along all material lines in the little less than five decades which have elapsed since then?

May I also add that, as I see it, it rests with Spokane, the queen city of the Inland Empire, to bring about a much greater development in the decades yet to come?

The people of the middle west, the east and the south are hungry for just such a wonderland as we possess in which to make their homes. If the citizens of Spokane will arise to the needs of advertising that counts, we can easily double the population of the entire Inland Empire in the next 25 years. But, you say: "How can this be done?"

I answer: "By word of mouth."

Pictures and circulars do not take the place of the personal touch.

CHAPTER V

A JAUNT TO ROCK LAKE

I had arranged for the coming of my sister, then in California, to act as my assistant in the school, but just prior to the opening of the fall term, she wrote that she had decided to marry instead of coming to Washington. This necessitated my beginning the year without an assistant. But I soon found the work too heavy and so employed Miss Nettie Ewart, one of my pupils.

This proved unsatisfactory. Nettie could do the work all right but some of the good people didn't like the idea of one of the pupils teaching their children. They wanted some one from outside to do the work.

After some weeks I learned that Miss Mary Davis of Leitchville was in town and that she had taught for several years in Walla Walla. I called to see her and she was glad to accept a position with me. This

47

interview resulted in her taking up the work on the first of January. My readers may be interested to know that I paid her $30 a month and board. This was good pay at that time. Teachers in the country schools were teaching for $40 a month.

We had a good year and enrolled more than a hundred students, many of them coming long distances and finding the best accommodations they could in the town. I always had from two to four girls with me in my little four-room house. That winter John C. Lawrence and Jonas Crumbaker of Garfield, rented my woodshed, a crude affair, which they papered with old newspapers. There they spent the winter, living principally on beans, in order that they might have the advantages the school afforded. Few young people of the present day would deny themselves in this way to secure an education.

Among the girls in my own home was Minnie Henderson, from the foot of Rock lake, whose brother had married Alice, a sister of Miss Davis. When it came time for the summer vacation, both of them were insistent that I should visit Rock Lake for a few days, prior to my taking up my itinerary in search of new pupils for the school.

This I consented to do. It is proper to add at this point that during the year I had made some money and so turned down an invitation from Professor Bayless to return to Dubuque and take up my work there. Three times during my life in Colfax this invitation was renewed and as many times turned down. I am no quitter.

Bright and early one beautiful June morning, we were in our saddles and turned our faces north and west to Rock Lake, 35 miles distant, a long ride after not having been in the saddle for a good many months. Some 15 miles out from town, I was riding ahead and noticed a company of Indians riding down the draw driving a band of cayuse ponies. As they came near, I called in a sociable tone of voice: "Hyu."

They responded, using the same word, and laughing uproariously, rode on. When Miss D. overtook me, I asked:

"Why did those Indians laugh at me?"

She wanted to know what I had said and when I told her, she laughed also. She said:

"Hyu means 'lots' and they, realizing that there was lots of you, took your word as a joke. You should have said 'clyhiem,' which means 'good morning.'"

It was midafternoon when we reached the Henderson mansion, which consisted of a single room 16 feet by 20 feet. Two corners were occupied by beds, a third by a cook-stove and the fourth by a table. In addition, there were a cradle, several chairs and benches, cooking utensils and a limited supply of dishes.

The family consisted of Henry Henderson, his wife, three children, the youngest a baby, and two hired men. During our stay, the hired men slept in the barn, a crude affair, built of logs with straw roof. Two nights, because of rain, we all had to sleep in the same room.

Now, it is all right after you get to bed, but decidedly awkward when making preparations for retiring and equally so in dressing in the morning. Pioneers soon learned to make the best of such minor difficulties. I have slept everywhere a person could sleep and eaten eveything one could eat and still be alive to tell the story.

I was tired after the long ride and found it more to my liking to rest standing up. The Hendersons were hospitable and we were soon much at home. Early the next morning, William Henderson, father of Henry and Minnie, rode over from his ranch several miles away and said that he had come to take us for a ride, in order that I might see the lake and its environment.

Although stiff and sore, I was soon in the saddle and headed for the head of the lake, the "Hole in the Ground," as it was called.

Rock Lake is formed by the Rock Creek which, leaving Bonnie Lake, flows for several miles through a woody section and then narrows to form a narrow gorge with a rather interesting waterfall. Here we find a number of acres of fairly level land, and in some mysterious fashion the water widens out and flows through a long defile between almost precipitous cliffs a distance of about eight miles. Then its waters are again confined to a narrow stream and it makes its way to the sea.

The lake is one-half mile in width at its widest point and of unknown depth. For the greater part of the lake, there is woodland on either side, but near the south end the land becomes more level and we find a number of farms, several of which are owned by the Henderson family.

A sawmill had been erected at the "Hole in the Ground," and reaching here about noon we were invited to dinner. Now I have had many invitations to dine, but this particular dinner stands out as unique. Yet it was seasoned with real genuine hospitality so characteristic of the pioneer.

The menu consisted of soda biscuits, adorned with yellow streaks, peas, potatoes and coffee. No meat, no milk, no butter! These people were surely vegetarians with a vengeance.

It was no uncommon thing at this time to find ranchers with many cows out on the range who had neither milk nor butter on their tables. It was too much trouble to milk a cow and to make butter.

One morning I suggested to Miss Davis that we ride over and make the DuBoises a visit. They lived a number of miles away on Rattlesnake, or Whisky, or Cabbage flat. At this late day I have forgotten which of these euphoniously named flats was theirs.

So I think we will call it "Cabbage," as the least harmful of the three.

George W. DuBois and his wife had come from somewhere in the East the year before and spent several weeks in Colfax. It was there I had become acquainted with them. They were cultured people and had given me a pressing invitation to visit them at their ranch home.

If my memory is not at fault, Mr. DuBois served in the territorial legislature from Whitman county at a later date. We found a most cordial welcome at their home. It didn't take any great amount of urging to induce us to spend a couple of days and nights with them. They were farming more after the fashion of the middle western farmer and were rapidly getting their land and buildings into proper shape for intensive production in the shortest possible time.

It was here I became acquainted with the immense vegetables which could be raised upon sod land. It was no uncommon thing to see potatoes which weighed five and six pounds. I saw one carrot which measured just six feet from the tips of its longest leaf to the end of its root.

I am really afraid to tell you of the turnips, cabbages and squashes which were raised, lest even you might be as skeptical as a woman who listened to me as I gave a public address at Lay Hill, Md., in 1895 on the resources of the great west from whence I came. Among other things I spoke of a great squash which had been on exhibition the fall before in Walla Walla and which weighed 136 pounds. This woman whispered to her neighbor and said: "That is a lie."

When I returned home I went to Mr. Ludwig, the grocer, and said:

"I want a big potato, the biggest you can find."

A few days later he delivered one that weighed a fraction over six pounds. This I put into a box and shipped to the storekeeper at Lay Hill. When I heard from my friend there some weeks later she said:

"You can come back to Lay Hill any time now and tell them whatever you choose. They will believe every word you say."

After a visit of about 10 days at Rock Lake we returned to Colfax. Miss Davis went to her home for the summer and it wasn't long until I was scouring the Palouse hills for pupils.

Late in July I rode out to Four Mile to spend a few days with Mrs. Williams, of whom I have already spoken. I found Father Stearns at home, and at the breakfast table the next morning he spoke of a family living across the mountain some six miles distant, where there were a young man and woman who might be induced to attend school in the fall. He further added:

"Now, you and Mrs. Williams can take my buckboard and get there in time for dinner and so meet them. I will keep house while you are away."

THE WIDE NORTHWEST

It was a glorious morning and we arrived about 11 o'clock at the Campbell home, where I was agreeably surprised to find a real mansion of three good-sized rooms. Mrs. C. wasn't expecting us, but we were made welcome and when she went out to a sod potato patch to secure a supply of that vegetable for our noonday meal I went with her.

She partly uncovered one hill and took therefrom a single potato which, when we had returned to the house, she prepared for dinner. Five people partook of the vegetable and there was enough left to fry for breakfast.

People from the effete east and middle west can not appreciate the wonders of our country in this respect. I remember years later when I was principal of the school at Rosalia having a man from Franklin, Ind., with his wife call upon me. While there he ridiculed the fabulous stories about our wonderful products. I excused myself, went to my garden and came back in a few minutes with a turnip which weighed just 10 pounds.

"Seeing is believing," he said: "I take it all back and will write to my paper. (He was an editor) and tell them the stories are not a bit exaggerated."

But to return to my subject, the young people were enrolled in my school that third and best year of my work in Colfax.

CHAPTER VI

A SECOND VISIT TO SPOKANE FALLS

When the school closed its third successful year I planned to take a trip of considerable length. My brother had married the previous fall and was located at Rosalia, where he had taken a homestead just west of the village. At this time they were living at the hotel and he was clerking in the store for Mr. Whitman, the owner, who had the stage station and hotel as well.

Mary Bowman, one of my 18-year-old school girls, was anxious to accompany me. To this I consented and one afternoon we mounted our cayuses and started for Cashup Davis' place, 14 miles north and six miles from Steptoe butte, where Mr. Davis was later to build a hotel and reside for a considerable period of time.

We found Mrs. Davis fat and jolly, and the girls, Mary, Annie and Charlotte, most delightful. The next morning, after a wonderful breakfast, I went to the store and asked Mr. Davis for my bill. He bristled up at once and said:

"Do you mean to insult me, Miss West?"

I responded:

"No, indeed, but I simply want to know how much I owe for this splendid entertainment."

Then he said:

"You don't owe me anything and any time the old maid school ma'am wants to come here and stop, she is more than welcome."

This illustrates the reception I received everywhere I went. Can you wonder I have in my heart a most kindly feeling for the old-time folk of the Inland Empire? My horse and I were always well cared for and given the best the place afforded.

May I digress and tell you how, many years later, I was visiting at the home of J. C. Lawrence, then in Garfield, when he said to me:

"Mrs. Jim Warmouth is camping in a cherry orchard six miles out of town and after supper we will drive out to see her."

After we left the carriage we had to walk a little distance over a plowed field. She saw us coming and recognizing me, hurried forward, put her arms around me and kissed me again and again, the tears running down her cheeks at the time. Her boys and girls were my pupils and I had visited in her home on Rebel flat many times.

Before the noon hour we were in Rosalia, where we found a gracious welcome. Here we spent two pleasant days and then moved northward, planning to spend another night with them on our return trip. I was greatly pleased with the choice of a wife my brother had made and have never had occasion to change my mind in the years since then. But this is not the chronicles of a family, and so I forbear further comment.

Some 10 miles farther north the Hale family had taken a homestead, and this was to be our next stop. Rose Hale, a charming young woman, had been my pupil and I had promised to make her a visit. When we arrived we found them with a comfortable two-room house, and Mr. Hale had gone to the mountains for fuel.

Mrs. H. at once captured and beheaded a chicken in our honor. When boiling water was needed for the scalding process it was discovered that, unlike husbands in these days, Mr. Hale had gone without leaving a suitable supply of fuel ready for the stove. It fell to my lot to saw and split the necessary wood for use during our stay with them. You can see by this that I am possessed of some really useful accomplishments.

After a delightful visit and a general searching for places of interest near at hand, we retired at a rather early hour, only to be aroused at midnight by Mrs. Hale coming to my bed and touching me on the shoulder. She whispered:

"Some one is trying to get into the house."

I arose at once, and in my night clothing, barefooted, seized the woman's weapon, a broom, and started around the house. The first time around I discovered nothing, but on making a second trip I found an old tomcat that had caused the disturbance. We retired and with minds at rest slept soundly until morning.

The next morning we moved on to Spokane Falls, a ride of nearly 30 miles. C. B. King and family had removed here, leaving his partner, Robert Ewart, in charge of the station at Colfax. Spokane had grown and was now a city of some 2,000 people. Of course, I found a home with Belle and her delightful family. They were always my good friends.

Years later, when he had purchased his 1600-acre ranch at Hayden Lake and erected a fine 16-room house, I was there on a camping trip with my brother and others. When I suggested one day that I should like to purchase a summer home on the lake shore, he said:

"You already have a summer home here, which you are welcome to occupy whenever you like."

Belle died many years ago and Mr. King about a year ago in Arizona. After four or five days here we rode on to Medical Lake for a visit with Flora (Stough) Wolfenden, who was running a small restaurant in the town.

Medical Lake had made considerable growth. There was a hotel and people were already beginning to go there for the medicinal properties of the water.

It is proper to say that Flora Stough had some

time previous to this married Frank Wolfenden, who was a competent young man, but erratic. Possibly a year after their marriage they were at the town of Sprague for a time. One night Frank arose in his night clothes and wandered down the railroad track. The next morning his body was found beside the track. It is supposed that he was temporarily deranged.

Flora's restaurant was a simple affair, just a single room, cheaply constructed. A calico curtain separated the kitchen and dining room. At night couches were prepared on the floor for sleeping purposes. I was used to this and so did not mind. The last I heard of her she was nearly blind and living in Minnesota. She had grown religious, which was entirely contrary to her nature.

After a pleasant visit with her, we rode on to Cheney, then beginning to be quite a town. Then Phenegar family from Colfax had removed here some time before and as May was one of my girls, we stopped for a little visit.

Cheney was the first county seat of Spokane county and held this proud distinction until 1886 when it was removed to Spokane Falls. There are those in the city today who claim that this honor never should have gone to Cheney but that is neither here nor there so far as my article is concerned. I have no wish to enter into any controversy upon this subject.

The streets of the town were simply footpaths, for

the most part among the stumps of the "primeval forest" which preceded human habitation. The town, as I remember it, owed its inception to the foresight of John C. Davenport, C. G. Linington and others from the city of Colfax.

I wonder sometimes if the people of Spokane city and county really realize how much they owe to these same Palousers, at whom, in the past, of course, some of our so-called "highbrows" were inclined to sneer. Much of the wealth and many of the far-sighted business men of the Palouse country aided materially in making Spokane what it is today and what it is destined to become in the future.

After a visit of 24 hours here, we turned our faces homeward. It was a warm, sunny morning and as we rode along, Mary said:

"I am so thirsty. I wish I had a drink."

Just then, I spied a small cabin in the woods near the roadside, and a bachelor out feeding his chickens and I replied:

"We will stop and ask that man for some water."

When we rode up and I had made known what we wanted, he took a tin cup and filling it with water from a spring near by handed it to me. I thanked him and passed the cup on to Mary, and she, poor girl, was obliged to at least make a pretense of drinking. (Excuse the illustration of one of Wilson's split infinitives.) The good bachelor had evidently used the

A SECOND VISIT

cup in which to mix his chicken feed, and had then forgotten to wash it.

When we arrived at Hale's we found the man of the house at home and we spent the night without the necessity of either chasing tomcats or splitting wood. As we left them and started upon our journey, I shall never forget the shock I experienced. As we rode along, we met a hack bound for Spokane containing Mrs. Whitman and the driver. They stopped and she told me that she and her husband had "agreed to disagree" and that she was leaving for the east. Thus in a few short days, I was to learn that a man and woman who had apparently lived together for many years in harmony were to separate and pursue different paths in life. This is such a common occurrence in this day that we pay no attention to it, but not so of the time of which I write.

A night at Rosalia, another at Cashup's and we were home again. My readers may like to know that the trip of more than 200 miles of riding and two weeks of time consumed (hold your breath) had cost me just one dollar and twenty-five cents. How does that compare with the cost of high living of the present day?

Another week of this vacation period was spent in the town of Moscow, Idaho, in attendance upon the sessions of the Mount Pleasant Baptist Association. I mention this because of the important bearing it had upon the future history of the school.

CHAPTER VII

A SCHOOL ENTERTAINMENT

Early in the summer, the Rev. S. W. Beaven, a son-in-law of the Rev. J. C. Baker, superintendent of missions for Oregon, Washington and north Idaho, arrived to take joint pastorates of Moscow and Colfax. He located with his family at Moscow but preached for us twice each month. He felt as I did that if the school was to grow as it should and accomplish its normal function to the community, it must have more and better equipment.

In June of this year, the Mount Pleasant Baptist Association met in Moscow. This brought delegates from the whole of Eastern Oregon, Idaho and Eastern Washington as well. Among the number was the Rev. D. J. Pierce of Walla Walla, a man of wide experience, and he, too, said:

"You must have more room and the school should be incorporated."

A SCHOOL ENTERTAINMENT

At the association which I attended, it was moved that they proceed at once to incorporate and that an effort should be made, headed by Mr. Beaven, to secure funds for the erection of an addition to the church, 28 feet by 32 feet, and two stories high, for the suitable housing of the growing school until such time as the denomination could see its way clear to erect a separate home for the institution.

At this gathering, highly eulogistic resolutions were passed commending me for my work in Colfax and urging the board, when created to retain me at the head of the school, if possible. Now, I am altogether too modest to reproduce these resolutions here. They are on record in the minutes of the association for that year.

The board of 15 members was duly organized and as I remember, James A. Perkins, the founder of Colfax, was made its president. I want to say that I never had a more loyal friend than he. He was a Congregationalist, broad-minded and interested in everything that had a tendency to upbuild the town. His wife, the oldest daughter of the Ewarts, and a most excellent woman, still survives.

Their two little daughters were members of my primary class. One day at the noon hour, as I stood conversing with some patron of the school, I noticed Minnie and Edna Sweet standing near. Minnie looked at me intently for a little time and then in a low tone of voice, I heard her say:

"Edna, isn't Miss West perfectly beautiful?"

I reached over and patting the child on the head said to the man with whom I was conversing:

"This is a real compliment, because, to her childish imagination I have been endowed, owing to my avoirdupois, with attributes which I do not possess."

Another event of this period had an important bearing upon the work of the school. Miss Davis, who had been my competent assistant, had been shot straight through the heart by that mysterious little personage called "Cupid," and so had decided that she must change her occupation in life and become Mrs. George W. Sutherland.

Now, while I have not been so fortunate as to be shot at by this little creature, I could not with any reasonable degree of justice withhold my consent. I was able, however, to secure as my assistant Miss Scott Montgomery, whose parents lived near Endicott at Matlock Bridge. Miss Scottie was a character in her way but proved to be a good teacher.

I remember a teachers' examination she took prior to her coming to work for me when the question was asked: "What are the uses of pain?" and she responded:

"To make us feel uncomfortable."

Of course, we could not allow her credits on such an answer, but she got through just the same.

This recalls another examination some 12 years ago when I, in three weeks' time, graded 5,000 pages of manuscript on physiology in Olympia. The wise author of the questions had asked:

"What is Fletcherism?"

Now, I felt that this was not a fair question and I marked it liberally, but when one lassie of Okanogan county said:

"There was a young maiden named Metcher,
Who forgot to study about Fletcher.
She took up her pen, put it down again—
"Next time I'll study you betcher."

She got full credit for her answer. A girl as bright as that would make a good teacher without a knowledge of Fletcher.

The school filled up rapidly and by the middle of the fall term, we had more than 100 on our rolls, nearly all young men and women. Mr. Beaven informed me that all the money needed for the addition had been subscribed except $150. I told him to go ahead with the building and the school would raise that amount.

The following Monday, I announced to the class that I was going to arrange for an entertainment to be given as soon as the new rooms were ready for us. We should have some literary exercises for which we should charge an admission fee of 25 cents. I would ask the ladies of the community to donate and serve a supper in the new school room for which we would charge 50 cents a plate. I further added that no pupil would be expected to pay for the meal, but none of the boys could take the school girls to supper.

I expected the girls to eat as many times as any one asked them to do so. Horatio Smith raised his hand and when given permission to speak said:

"But there isn't a girl in town who isn't in the school."

I remarked that the girls had mothers.

"You boys will eat free of charge but you must pay for some one of the mothers," I said.

Nobly did the girls rise to the importance of the occasion. Some of them ate three times that night, while the boys each had to part with 50 cents but their own meal was free, and such a meal. It makes me hungry this minute to think of it.

The eventful night arrived. We presented a really good program. The church had a seating capacity of 125. We took in $55 at the door and I have never known how they all managed to get in. Those who had parts in the exercises had been told that when they were free, they could go around the building and slip in, but they were unable to find seats and so filled the windows on the outside and simply looked in.

Just as the exercises closed I came out and announced the supper and added:

"I shall be at a candy stand here in the corner at my left, prepared to cheat you to the best of my ability. The first man to come to the stand was John C. Davenport and he said:

A SCHOOL ENTERTAINMENT

"Well, Miss West, it is the first time in my life I was told ahead of time that I was to be cheated, and here I am as "a lamb to the slaughter." Go ahead and do your worst."

He handed me a silver dollar. I gave him five or six pieces of candy and kept the change.

Ben Burgunder, a merchant of the town and later my "son-in-law," for he married Dora Lansdale, who was one of my finest girls, made arrangement with Oliver Hall, for many years a dignified state senator from Whitman county, to take me to dinner while he stole a box of candy. Of course, I accepted Oliver's invitation and, calling Scottie to the stand, we entered the dining room.

Inside of five minutes Burgunder came in and treated us each to some of my finest candy. When I returned to the stand I asked:

"How much candy did Mr. Burgunder buy?" I was informed that he had made no purchase. I suspected as much, and so called a boy and sent Mr. B. a bill for $5 for candy purloined. He made haste to come and remonstrate, saying it wasn't worth more than 40 cents.

I admitted the fact, but said:

"You stole it and so must stand the consequences of your wrong doing."

I finally let him off on payment of $2.50. In about two hours I had sold out candy and nuts which cost me some $17 for about $50. It was in this way that I outshylocked Shylock.

Mr. Delano, the butcher, who had a son in school, took a large ham, boiled it, then removing the skin and fat, he took it to the bakery and had it frosted and decorated with my name, the date and with a big red rose in the center. It made a wonderfully beautiful table decoration and I wouldn't allow them to cut it. In fact, I kept it so long that it spoiled and I had to throw it away.

I shall always have a warm corner in my heart for the good women who helped me so royally in the affair. When it was all over and the cost counted, we had almost $150 and the deficit was soon made up by my friends.

I need not say that my reputation was made as a candy seller. In a few weeks the Methodist people gave a social and I was invited to take charge of the candy stand. I consented, but said:

"You know my conscience will not allow me to make more than 100 per cent profit for a church."

They had to be satisfied with that.

Then along came the Congregational folk and proffered the same request and I doubled their money invested. I really have a conscience, even though it may be seared at times.

It was a great comfort to have more room. I engaged Miss Mary Shaw, an old pupil, as my primary teacher, and we closed a most satisfactory year with all bills paid and a little balance on hand. I now notified the board that Professor Bayless had sent me a second invitation to return to my old post in Iowa. The folks were anxious I should remain in Colfax.

They were quite ready to make all kinds of promises and finally I said:

"If you will relieve me of all collections, payment of teachers, all business connected with the work and pay me a reasonable salary, I will remain at least for another six months and will look after the general government of the school and the teaching.

This they readily promised to do. I turned down my Iowa offer for the second time.

But I was to learn that even these good people found it much easier to promise than to fulfill. I was obliged to go on just as I had been doing in the past years of the work. In the final article of this series I want to tell you of my concluding work in Colfax and my change of base from private to public school training.

It is due to my readers to know that J. Orin Oliphant of the Cheney normal told me several nights ago that he had compared all matters of history in my articles with the files of the Palouse Gazette of corresponding date and that they tally exactly.

CHAPTER VIII

REVEREND CUSHING EELLS

When Oliver Goldsmith, in describing his own father in "The Village Preacher," said:

"A man he was to all the country dear,

"And passing rich with forty pounds a year," he most delightfully portrayed the character of one who was to live several generations later in the person of the Rev. Cushing Eells, the pioneer missionary to the Indians of the Northwest. I wish I might paint for you such a vivid picture of this truly good and great man as I knew him in the years 1878-81, that he might become to you the inspiration his life has been to me since that period.

Imagine, if you please, a man of medium size, with hair and beard mostly gray; the beard carefully trimmed, the hair so smooth one could almost imagine he used the "stacomb" of the present day; a kindly, benevolent face, a rather keen penetrating eye, in which lurked a quiet determination which fully indicated the character of the man. He was not easily swerved from his purpose.

When you looked into his face you knew instinctively:

"Here is a truly good and honorable gentleman."

The apostle Paul made no mistake when he said:

"Ye are living epistles known and read of men."

The Rev. Cushing Eells possessed that peculiar thing we call "personality" at the present day to a marked degree.

In the fall of 1878 he was elected school superintendent for Whitman county and soon after he took office he came to me and said:

"Miss West, I am an old man. My methods are more or less antiquated, but you are young and up to date in your work. Will you help me out?"

I accepted the appointment so graciously tendered and we spent two delightful years of service together. I have in the autograph album to which I have already alluded a page on which he wrote.

"The generous deeds of Miss L. L. West will be held in grateful remembrance.—Cushing Eells."

While this is to be a biographical sketch of Father Eells only in so far as my relations with him are concerned, yet I can not refrain from giving you a glimpse of his mode of life at this period. He built for himself a shack near the Congregational church, which he erected, giving dollar for dollar received from any one else. I have been told he did the same for a number of churches in the Inland Empire. It is certain that he gave a bell to each church built while he was on the field.

The shack was built of upright boards, shiplapped on the outside, and consisted of a single large room with attic overhead where he slept. This attic was reached by a series of slats nailed to the wall in the leanto on the north side of the building where he kept his saddle and feed for his well-beloved horse, Le Blond (French for sorrel horse).

This horse, by the way, was his companion in all his trips from 1874 to 1888. With him he crossed the Cascade mountains three different times. The historical society of Tacoma has had the horse embalmed and he's on exhibition in their museum. Mrs. J. A. Perkins of Colfax is my authority for this statement.

There being no county offices at this time, Father Eells kept the records in his home. I must tell you of the interior of this mansion. There were a large box, stove, a table, roughly made, several rawhide bottomed chairs, a bench or two and along the east end of the room a long bookcase filled with books mostly theological.

During his frequent absences from town, I had the key to the premises in case I might need something in the way of school material. Now, I am of an inquiring turn of mind and I wanted to see where he slept, so one day during his absence, I climbed the slat stairway, already mentioned, and looked into his sleeping apartment. There were two nail kegs in the room upon which rested a board some 18 inches wide. Upon this board he spread his blankets and with his saddle bags for a pillow, secured his needed rest. There was absolutely no other furniture in the room.

Can you imagine a 75-year-old man living in such discomfort today? He told me himself that his food cost him on the average just 37 cents a week. He drank neither tea nor coffee and milk only occasionally.

I happened to have occasion to call at his home one morning on my way to school, for I had moved into a home on the hill that spring, on a matter of business and found him just eating his breakfast. I consisted of fried onions and a bread he made from several kinds of flour (white, cornmeal and graham) mixed with a little salt and water and baked in a frying pan on top of his stove.

We remonstrated with him many times for being so abstemious but he always answered:

"I have enough to keep me well and there is too great need for me to spend my money for luxuries."

Nor would he eat anything but the plainest food when invited to our homes, as he often was. I remember his coming to my house one time just as we were sitting down to our noonday meal. I insisted upon his eating with us.

Now, it happened that it was Saturday and I had just purchased a box of beautiful tomatoes from Snake River. He partook heartily of the food and when he left he said:

"May I have one of those beautiful tomatoes?" I said:

"Yes, Father Eells, you may have them all if you want."

He would only take two and I saw to it they were the finest in the box. This is the only time I ever knew him to ask for anything in the line of food.

He sometimes visited my school for a little time to observe my methods of teaching. On one occasion I was teaching cube root, then receiving much more attention than at present. I always used the geometric method of explanation, using blocks that my good friend, Oliver Hall, had made for me. Father Eells had never seen it before and was very much interested. When I had concluded the explanation, he asked me to repeat it which I did first with two figures in the root and then with three. He said:

"That is wonderful. I never really understood cube root before."

It made such an impression upon him that later when we held our first institute, he insisted upon my making the same explanation to the teachers, after which he admonished them to learn the method, and if they could not afford to buy blocks to make them out of a potato.

Just prior to the first teachers' examination in the spring, he came to me and said:

"The law requires that I must call to my assistance two teachers holding first-grade certificates and there is not a first-grade teacher in the county. Let me see your Iowa certificate."

I showed him one granted me several years before and with a sigh of apparent relief he said:

"Well, that is satisfactory and we shall have to do the work by ourselves."

At the examination, we granted three first-grade certificates to John C. Lawrence, Harvey Irwin and R. O. Hawks, who went to Dayton to teach soon after.

Two days before the examination, he came to me with the questions and said:

"The law requires that these questions be opened in the presence of the class, but I know I can trust you and I am asking you to take the questions and answer them just as you would if you were taking the test, that I may have them as a guide in grading manuscripts."

Let me say in explanation as to the need for this that on account of my school, I could only assist him out of school hours.

THE WIDE NORTHWEST

We held our first county teachers' institute just prior to the May examinations in 1880. There were present about 30 of the teachers of the county. I acted as secretary and also took a considerable part in the teaching of methods to those present.

I remember reading a paper at this institute in which I said that the time was coming in the near future when instead of teaching technical grammar, so-called, we would stress the teaching of language, how to talk and write correctly. They laughed me to scorn, but inside of 20 years, we were doing just that thing in all our schools.

This leads me to say that soon after I began my work in Walla Walla I read another paper in which I said we were coming to the time when we should teach sewing, carpentering, etc., etc., in our public schools. Again I was laughed to scorn, but within 25 years, we were doing just that also, and while I am neither a prophet nor the child of a prophet, I could tell you some other things that are bound to come to pass before our schools measure up to the point of efficiency which they must attain in the not distant future.

Father Eells was always just in the smallest particular. Until the summer of 1879, my school room was used for all religious services held in the town. When both the Methodists and Congregationalists had so far completed their houses of worship that they could be used, the Sunday school continued to be held in the Baptist church until four years later when

REVEREND CUSHING EELLS

I resigned as superintendent and immediately three Sunday schools were organized.

In the spring of the year just mentioned, Father Eells came to me and asked:

"Who has been paying for fuel consumed and janitor work for our services during the winter?"

When I told him I had, he said:

"This must not be." At his next appointment, he presented the matter to the congregation and at the close of the service turned over to me $20. While this did not cover the whole expense, it was a help.

In the summer of this year he handed me a county warrant for my work as his deputy and when I refused to accept he said in his slow deliberate fashion:

"Miss West, you have it in your power to be of great assistance to me in the future but if you will not accept remuneration therefor, I can not call on you."

This put an entirely different phase on the matter and so I accepted the warrant. The next year, instead of offering to pay me, he made a trip to Portland during the summer and the morning the fall term of school began he brought to the school, and hung a beautiful eight-day clock, started it, and then turning to me said:

"This is your personal property but I request that you use it in the school while you remain here."

As I watched its slow, deliberate beat of the pendulum and the almost inaudible tick, I said:

"It is just like you, Father Eells."

He responded:

"I just hate a clock that goes tick, tick."

I kept the clock for many years and then before leaving Walla Walla. I made a present of it to Whitman College, knowing that that disposition of it would be pleasing to him. My pupils had ere this given me a handsome clock and I had no need for two.

In his long trips about the country, he was accustomed to put in his saddle bags a supply of his peculiar bread, and with his blankets he started out, stopping at night beside a stream of water and hobbling his horse, he ate his frugal repast, rolled up in his blankets and lying on the hard ground, slept till morning.

In the fall of 1894, when an effort was being made to raise money to help to keep Whitman college on its feet, I wrote and published in a Walla Walla paper the following lines inscribed to his memory:

"Broad-minded, noble Christian man:
  "Large-hearted; generous! Can you find
"In all the world since time began
  "A life more true, a heart more kind
"Than throbbed within his aged breast—
  "A heart that beat in sweet accord
"With yours and mine and all the rest
"Who render homage to the Lord?"

CHAPTER IX

SOME NOTABLE PUPILS OF THE COLFAX PERIOD

In the days of the old Roman empire, the mother was lauded as the important factor in the development of good and patriotic Roman citizens. What was true then is equally true today. The mother is without a doubt the factor which rules the world in this enlightened twentieth century. I want to "take off my hat," figuratively speaking, to the young women who went to school to me at Colfax and who have become wives and mothers.

I can award you no greater praise than this. It will be impossible to name you all in this brief sketch but I want to say, I am intensely proud of you even though you are not enrolled in the rather peculiar product of our times. "The New Woman."

I am also proud of the fact, that so far as I am informed, few of the young men and women of that early day went wrong. I read some years ago of a mythical school master who, after a long period of years, stated that not one of his boys ever went wrong. I can not say the same because I know for a fact that two of my boys were incarcerated in the penitentiary for horse stealing and one of the girls proved not to be what is regarded as quite respectable in polite society.

But, I am sure I can say without fear of contradiction, that fully 95 per cent of the student body made upright, honorable citizens of our great country. The mantle of charity shall cover those who fell by the wayside.

But there have been a few who, because of environment, aggressiveness of character, superior foresight, and what not, have made for themselves names in the business, professional, or political world. I am so fortunate as to present to my readers the names of some of these. It is a singular fact that, so far as I know, not one of them with a single exception ever became a minister of the gospel, and he an Adventist.

This may have been because my example did not tend to piety in the life of the individual pupil. I might not have thought of this except for the fact that a prominent citizen of this city said to me soon after I began writing this series that he was ashamed of me in that I would tell over my own signature of the "Old Adam" lurking in me which prompted my doing such atrocious things as getting even with a Dayton landlord.

In this day of the "New Woman," it is not necessary to mention the ladies first as in the olden time, so I

shall begin with the men and the name of one now
of sacred memory shall head the list.

Horatio Smith came to me from the Snake River
country, a boy of about 15 and a really noble fellow,
as his after life abundantly proved. He was a boy
of one idea and he had decided prior to this what he
wanted to do. He came to me with the request that
I allow him to pursue just such studies as would best
fit him for that life. When he had completed his al-
gebra he felt he ought to have some geometry, and
while it was my policy never to organize a new class
unless at least three students desired to pursue the
special study, I allowed him to take up the study
and for some months heard him recite out of school
hours.

Soon after he left school, he became a locomotive
engineer and because of circumstances over which he
had no control, he was satisfied to give up his higher
ambition and continued in this vocation until he was
obliged to give up work just a few months ago. No
finer son, no truer husband, no better father, no more
loyal friend, no more patriotic citizen ever lived than
Horatio Smith. His memory must ever be a bene-
diction to all of us who knew and loved him for his
sterling character. Such men make the world better
for having lived in it.

In the fall of 1878 in a certin eastern Oregon wheat
field, as a company of men sat upon a lot of grain
sacks, one of them, a boy of 18, picked up a copy
of the Palouse Gazette which some one had dropped

and read aloud the fact that an academy was soon to be started in the town of Calfax. He then said:

"Boys, I am going to Colfax and go to school to that 'old maid.'"

In May, 1879, at the time of the first teachers' examination as I came into the room where the examination was being held and surveyed the group of young people, victims of this examination, I said to Father Eells:

"Who is that verdant looking young man in the corner?"

He replied:

"Wait until you see the papers of that green young man."

It was to him that a first grade certificate was awarded with the highest grade, up to that date, ever given in the county. That young man was John C. Lawrence. He went to school to me for three winters thereafter, teaching in the summer to defray his expenses.

I never had a better pupil nor one I regarded more highly. By the time he was 21 he was county superintendent of schools, then territorial superintendent for two years, a banker, member of the first state legislature, register of the land office at Waterville, a member of the railroad commission and an unsuccessful candidate for governor on the progressive ticket as a follower of Roosevelt. He is now managing a co-operative egg and poultry plant at Winlock, Wash.

SOME NOTABLE PUPILS

In a letter of late date from A. L. Davenport, now president of the Pacific Lumber Company of Aberdeen, Wash., he says:

"I have much to thank you for, as you gave me my initial start toward a more or less successful business career. Many of the pupils thought I was your favorite, I think, because you used to say at a certain time each day:

" 'Link, please pass the ink.'

"This was a distinction of which I was proud."

Link is one of the fine business men of our state today.

One of four brothers, all of whom were my pupils, Dr. George A. Chapman, studied dentistry and has been for years a resident of Colfax where he has built up by his own energy and skill a good practice.

When Dr. Harvey Felch, Ellensburg, sent me his picture he said:

"For your 'rogues' gallery.' "

Those of us who know Harvey and his many patients as well are sure he is one of the really great men in his chosen calling.

Walter A. Holt, one of the splendid boys of pioneer days and I think the youngest of his family, found his way to Portland and entered the employ of Wells-Fargo National Bank of that city. This is now one of the strongest institutions of its kind and is today the

U. S. National Bank of Portland. He is vice-president.

About the time of my arrival in Colfax there came to the town a Mr. Bellinger, an agricultural implement dealer. He was a big man, physically as well as mentally. I do not remember ever seeing a broader back on a human being than he possessed. There were five children in the family: Blanche, who married many years ago Judge Joseph Sessions of Davenport; Will, the eldest boy, who resides in Honolulu; Elmer, in the same business as his father and Caddie, while Lawrence is the senior member of the firm of Bellinger & Burrows, automobile dealers of this city. They were all my pupils and a fine lot of young people.

I attended one of the last meetings of the territorial association for teachers in Spokane. While here, I was invited to dinner and to spend the night with Mrs. H. C. Blair, formerly Maggie Inman, an old pupil. After dinner she took me to ride in northeast Spokane, where there were few houses at that time, and while we were out she said:

"I have been thinking of the three years I went to school to you in Colfax and there is not a single unpleasant incident connected with all that time. It was just a happy dream."

Then I laughed and said:

"We human beings are so constituted that with the lapse of time we forget the unpleasant things that come to us in life and remember only the pleasant features."

Mrs. Blair is so well known in Spokane for her public school and business college work that I have no need to eulogize her. She is now an invalid and is confined to her wheel chair, but she is bright and cheerful and always glad to see her friends. (She is now deceased.)

Mary Kennedy, now Mrs. Liddle, has had a remarkable career. She is still a resident of Colfax. Her home has been destroyed by fire on two different occasions and again by flood; her husband was an invalid for a long time prior to his death; she has been for years a clerk and is now deputy auditor. She has kept sweet and happy through it all.

Mamie James, whose father, ex-governor of Nebraska and register of the United States land office in Colfax, made a record for herself as a compositor. She later married, becoming the wife of Ivan Chase, the editor of the Palouse Gazette. It was he, if I remember correctly, who changed the name of the paper to the Colfax Gazette.

They have two grown sons and were until recently connected with the state training school for boys at Chehalis. Mr. Chase had charge of the boys' print shop. Olney, the eldest son was chief probation officer of the institution but has resigned.

I have just heard that Minnie Holt Muir, a sister of Walter Holt, is at the girls' training school at Grandmound, much loved by the inmates. They have come to call her "Aunt Minnie." By an interesting coincidence, these three girls, Mary Kennedy, Mamie James and Minnie Holt, went to school to me that first day in Colfax so many years ago. Thus we are able to catch a glimpse of the wide influence that primitive school is exerting upon the present-day world.

Then there were the Rice boys, Eugene, his mother's chief comfort, and Bert, who was inclined to be something of a torment, just a typical boy, if you please.

There was in my school for a considerable period of time one Louis P. Bauman of German extraction. Now, Louis had all the plodding industry of his ancestors and he proved to be a most excellent and exemplary young man. Later the family moved to Spokane where he became associated with the Centennial Milling Company in a rather humble way at first. Today he is secretary and treasurer of the company with headquarters in Seattle. I have heard it whispered that he is one of the heavy stockholders in the concern. Jonas Crumbaker, the boy who spent the winter in my woodshed with John Lawrence, married soon after leaving school. He has been for years a smalltown hardware man in Garfield. His most notable achievement, however, is not in business. Like Roosevelt, he is a believer in large families. I am not sure whether it is seven or nine children who have come to bless his home.

SOME NOTABLE PUPILS

Then the Warner boys, Elmer, George Emerson and Herbert. Elmer married one of his classmates, Mary Steward. George died and Emerson and Herbert are among the good business men of Seattle today.

Will Langdon, whose father, W. W. Langdon, was our first tinner in Colfax, is now a successful business man in Walla Walla, being associated with his brother, John, in many enterprises. I have always been sorry that I could not claim John as one of my boys except in an adopted sense. He was too young to go to school when the family was in Colfax. I had the privilege, however, of teaching Nell, the youngest of the family, but that is another story and belongs to the Walla Walla period.

I must not forget D. F. Staley, now a prominent business man and banker of Pullman, nor Homer King who I have learned is a newspaper writer in California. In a letter recently received from him, he says, "We have our memories and mine of you lie so close to the beginning of life's trail, when life was all joy, that I hold them near sacred."

Signed your humblest child, Homer B. King.

CHAPTER X

SOME INTERESTING INCIDENTS

It is the unexpected which gives real zest to life and makes it worthwhile from a human standpoint. This is entirely aside from the thought of so many people that our activities here are simply preparation for that higher and better existence in the world to come. Be that as it may, in this article I simply narrate some of the minor events which were part and parcel of my life in Colfax.

Soon after the beginning of school there came to the hotel Dr. Plyley and his wife. The doctor was a big, blustering sort of fellow, who was inclined to be irascible by nature, while his wife was a meek, pretty little woman, much dominated by her lordly husband. This is, I suppose, as it should be, judging from the writings of St. Paul on the subject. It was he who wrote: "Let wives be in subjection to their own husbands."

88

INTERESTING INCIDENTS

The doctor had come to town to engage in the practice of his profession. Not long after their arrival, he came into the parlor late one evening where Mrs. W. H. Davenport and I sat conversing and said:

"My wife has accidentally taken poison. Will you ladies come and help me out?"

We could do nothing else but comply with his request. About 2 a. m. the effects of the poison had been counteracted and we bade them good night.

A couple of days later I met him in the hall sporting a new suit of clothes and I remarked:

"Well, doctor, you look pretty fine this morning."

Drawing himself up to his full height, he said:

"You do not know me well or you would know I dress this well every day."

I thanked him for the rebuke and moved on. One morning I went down to breakfast a little early and just after me the doctor and his wife came in and took the table adjoining mine. Birdie Piper, the waitress, came and took their order.

After a short delay she came with their breakfast but in the meantime the doctor had worked himself up into a towering rage and turning to Birdie as she placed the food on the table he made some uncomplimentary remarks.

She, with her quick temper, for she was red-headed, answered back, but saying nothing really disrespectful. This only angered him the more and with an oath he said:

"I shall report you to the landlady."

Just at this juncture, Mrs. Ewart entered the room and took a seat some distance away. Dropping his napkin the doctor jumped up and started to make his complaint and I followed him. After he had unburdened himself, I said:

"Mrs. Ewart, I witnessed the affair and heard every word said and I want to tell you that Birdie was in no way to blame. It was only a fit of ill-temper on the part of the doctor."

Of course, he didn't feel kindly toward me—I am telling this story simply to show upon what a flimsy foundation fame sometimes rests for ere.

Ere the close of the day it was reported on the street that Dr. Plyley had slapped Birdie Piper at breakfast that morning and that I had taken a chair and knocked him down. It was thus I gained celebrity as a pugilist. Not long thereafter the Plyleys "folded their tent and quietly stole away." It is interesting to note that Birdie later married Dick Wright, they lived for a long time at Rathdrum and then at Hayden Lake.

In February, 1879, we had high water and for some days there was grave danger of the town being flooded. A woman with a small child came in on the stage and was stranded in the town for several days. She was given the room off the parlor and adjoining that of Leon Kuhn. I had the room directly overhead.

INTERESTING INCIDENTS

Now, sounds were distinctly audible in the boarding houses of that day. One night the child was troublesome and cried a good deal. After a time Mr. Kuhn called:

"Keep that ———— young one still."

The next morning at breakfast I told him that I was ashamed of him, and he said:

"Sis, you shall never hear me swear again." I never did.

One Sunday night it was stormy and there being no church a lot of us gathered in the parlor for singing, story-telling and other forms of amusement. Dr. P. D. Bunnel, his wife, and some others had come in for the evening.

Mr. Kuhn had a company of men in his room and I suppose got tired of our noise and chatter. They began to sing what we would call jazz music today. After a few minutes of this I got angry and rang the bell. When the boy came from the office, I said:

"Tell Captain Ewart I want him in the parlor."

The boy evidently knew what was the trouble for instead of coming himself the captain sent a note to Mr. K. saying:

"The parlor complains."

Then we were regaled for a time with speculations as to the nature of the disease called "parlor complaint." Our guests left and the men in Mr. K.'s room passed out of the window to the balcony and so downstairs.

But Mr. K. came alone through the parlor and just before he reached the door leading into the hall he turned, and looking directly at me said:

"And so you were mad, were you?"

Then the vials of my wrath opened upon him. I have no idea just what I said but those present told me my eyes snapped fire and they never listened to such a tirade of rebuke as he received. He listened quietly and then said:

"Thank you."

Leaving the room, he went to the office where he told the men what I said. He told them it wouldn't have been so bad had there not been others present to hear it; that not even his own mother had ever talked to him as I did. Then he remarked that he would like to put me into a cannon and shoot me over the hill.

In the morning my anger had evaporated and I met him in the hall with a pleasant "Good morning," but he didn't see me at all; nor did either he or Mr. Lippitt occupy their seats at the breakfast table.

This state of affairs continued for several weeks. I always spoke when we met and he ignored my presence. Finally one night, much to my surprise, the names of Mr. Lippitt and Mr. Kuhn were presented for membership in the Good Templars lodge.

INTERESTING INCIDENTS

This was an indication of surrender for when we went forward to welcome the new members after their initiation he shook hands cordially, walked home with me, visited for a while in the parlor and the next morning, both men were in their old places in the dining room.

When some one in passing made a joking remark about them being there Mr. K. said:

"Sis and I kissed and made up last night."

When he married Frankie Ewart some time later, I was a guest by his special invitation and he was always accounted one of my choice friends to the day of his death. This true story has an important moral. Can you find it?

In the early spring of the year, Father Stearns who, you will remember, had been the means of my taking up the work in Colfax, visited the school. There were nearly 100 young men and women present. After he had listened for a while I asked the school to lay their work aside, and introducing Father Stearns, invited him to address the class.

He stood and smilingly looked the young people over and then said, much to my dismay: "All you young people who love your teacher stand up."

Of course, they all stood up. They could do nothing else. I have been mighty careful ever since how I asked people to speak to my school.

But I was not to have a clear field for my enterprise. In the fall of 1881 some good people, I have never known just who they were decided that because of the meager public school equipment of the town, there was need for a second private enterprise.

"Competition is the life of trade." They desired to apply the same principle to school work. In October, Adrian Wisner opened a private school, charging $5 a quarter for instruction, much less than my charges, and expected, I suppose, to take a number of my pupils to the cheaper school. He failed in this and soon sold the enterprise to Henry Sullivan. At the close of the fall term they had fifteen pupils and I had 100.

The winter term began with a full school and, much to my surprise I enrolled among my pupils May Sullivan, a sister, and May Hudson a step-sister of my competitor, both of them fine girls. They at once paid ten dollars to apply on tuition for the term. Two weeks later when school was dismissed in the afternoon I noticed the two Mays were still in their seats. When I inquired what was wanted they came forward and told me that inasmuch as I had so many pupils and brother Henry so few their parents thought best that they should drop out of the Academy and go to the brother. They assured me again and again of their sorrow for the step but of course they had to go.

This was simply a scheme to cause a stampede from my school to the smaller institution, but it signally failed, as not a single pupil except the two girls mentioned dropped out.

INTERESTING INCIDENTS

Soon after the school was incorporated Judge W. A. Inman, one of the trustees, attended one of our Friday afternoon rhetorical exercies, I invited him to speak, and after eulogizing my work and expressing the greatest confidence in my ability to teach, he nearly took my breath away by remarking that it was the plan of the board as soon as possible to secure some good man to take over the work, and make the school a real success. Some folks were inclined to resent this, but I laughed and said: "This is simply the attitude of the great mass of the people, they think that only a man can accomplish anything worth while.

Now, I am not telling this story out of any disrespect to the good Judge who was, to the day of his death my good friend, nor to his daughter one of my best girls but simply to show the feeling of people of that time, and to some extent of the present time that it takes a man to bring about the greatest success along any line of human endeavor.

One more story and I am done. One day Edna Sweet came to me with a small sum of money and asked me to keep it for her till noon. I dropped it in my desk and went on with my work. I was called out during the noon hour and when just before the opening in the afternoon, Edna came for her money it was gone. Now, I had about a hundred young people in the school and I called attention to the theft and said: "I do not want to believe that there is a thief among your number. I have reimbursed Edna for her loss and shall absent myself from the room for several days at the noon hour, or until the money is returned. It never was but a good many years afterwards, I had a letter from a young man who was my janitor at the time stating that he saw me drop the money in the desk and he coveted it, and during my absence took it from my desk, he was then afraid to return it fearing some one might see him put it back. He had now been converted and wanted to join the Adventist Church but could not do so until he had made restitution.

I have had several experiences of the same nature in my work but one is sufficient to show what a real conversion will accomplish in this respect.

CHAPTER XI

CLOSING WORK IN COLFAX

At Christmas time in 1904 the Shaw-Borden Company of this city published for me 1500 copies of a beautiful little booklet which I sent during the winter to my old pupils and a few other people. This book contained a chapter of pioneer life and some poems which I had written from time to time. Soon after it was sent out I had a letter from my sister, now deceased, saying that she was pleased with the book, but suggested that she would have liked it better if I had used the first personal pronoun, singular, instead of the plural form.

In accordance with this criticism, in the sketches I am now writing I am making them personal by the use of the first person singular whenever possible.

As I review the work, however, I am reminded of a story which illustrates how I feel about it. Bill and Sal were pioneers. They had taken a homestead on

97

the frontier, erected a one-room log cabin and cleared a small plot of land. One day while they were at dinner a huge brown bear ambled into the room through the open door.

Bill immediately jumped to a place of comparative safety upon a joist supporting the roof, but Sal snatched up an ax and dispatched Mr. Bruin. When assured that their unwelcome guest was really dead, Bill descended just in time to throw out his chest and remark to a neighbor who just then appeared:

"See what a big bear me and Sal killed."

Now for the application.

The splendid pioneer men and women who stood by me so faithfully are Sal. The school is the defunct bear which, though dead, yet speaketh through its fine student body while "Me" is the writer of this article and those which preceded it.

But unlike the cowardly Bill, I do not arrogate to myself the whole glory of achievement but am more than glad to divide the honor with those who so loyally upheld my hands. Be this my excuse for using "I" so often. It really means "we" and includes the whole constituency of the school.

Although I had consented to remain in Colfax another six months, I decided to give up my home and board. This I secured in the home of the Rev. George Campbell, the newly arrived Baptist minister, whose wife was a skilled musician and proved to be a most competent assistant in that line. Miss Lucy Spaulding was employed to assist with the advanced work while Mary Shaw still had charge of the primary department.

In this connection I want to mention a man who, with his family, was a real godsend to a struggling school such as I was conducting. Some time prior to my arrival, Nelson Davis, a widower, with 11 children, met and married a Mrs. Steward, a widow, and the mother of 11 "olive branches."

I never had a more loyal supporter of the school than Mr. Davis and I delight to accord him honor. There was never a time when I had none of the family in the student body, and for a good deal of the time, eight of the children attended school at the same period.

He, in fact, furnished the wood for the school and I paid for it in tuition. The 23d child of this remarkable family was born during my life in Colfax. She now teaches in the Spokane city schools. It was my privilege just a few days ago to meet and talk with his daughter, Mrs. Jessie (Davis) Slate, who resides in Colfax and is the mother of nine children.

The school filled up rapidly and ere many weeks, I had ninety of the finest young people to be found anywhere in my school.

There would have been more than I could handle but the Methodists had recently opened a college in

Spokane which naturally took a good number from that region of my territory.

Our treasurer, Thomas Kennedy, was a fine young man, but he was busy with his own affairs and so, I was perforce obliged to send out my own bills, make collections, pay my teachers and such other bills as were necessary in conducting the enterprise. By the end of the second term, I was able to meet all bills, including my own salary, and turned over to Mr. Kennedy something like $50 still due the school from tuitions.

In February, 1883, I had a letter from President Bayless for the third and last time, making me a most advantageous offer if I would return to my old position in Dubuque. He gave me until October first to get there, if I desired that much time.

I replied that I was due in Olympia as a member of the territorial board of education in April and then thought I should go to California to visit relatives for a time, and its was likely that I should accept his offer but this was not to be.

The reason therefore will be narrated in a series of sketches to follow at a later date. Some one has wisely said:

"We see not a step before us.
  "God hangs a mist o'er our eyes.
"And before each step of our onward way;
  "He makes new scenes to arise."

THE WIDE NORTHWEST

After long years of experience, I am sure that we can not know for a certainty just what is ahead of us in the future.

The winter passed quietly and pleasantly, and when the springtime came and I bade goodby to many kind friends and closed my life chapter of private school teaching. In the decades since I have always been associated with our glorious public school system, which, in spite of its many faults, is still the pride and glory of our great American commonwealth.

You will remember that in a former article I referred to the fact that the county seat question of this county was permanently settled and Spokane became for all time our capital town.

Just after I had taken that article to the printer I received from a friend the following transcript from our county records. Believing it to be of real interest to our people, I submit it just as it came to me:

"Territory of Washington: Territorial cases, 58 and 71. Ex. rel. Harker, plaintiff; versus W. H. Bishop, defendant, and Robert Crawford and J. N. Glover, intervenors.

"From the above cases in the office of the county clerk of Spokane county, I found the following:

"At the election held on November 2, 1880, to determine whether or not the county seat should be moved from Spokane Falls, where it was then located, the following votes were cast, as shown in the district court journal, "A" pages 35, 42, 43, 45, 46, 48, 51.

"Cheney, 680.

"Spokane Falls, 575.

"Sprague, 19.

"Spangle, 12.

"Medical Lake, 1.

"Marshall, 2.

"In the night time of the days of March 21 and 22, 1881, the county auditor took all the records and removed them to the town of Cheney. For several years after that the above cases were fought in the court of the state. In the fall of 1886 the records were returned to the courthouse in Spokane Falls by a body of citizens that never made their identity known.

"The following were officers at that time: J. T. Lockheart, clerk; W. H. Bishop, auditor; S. C. Wingard, judge of the district court and associate justice of the supreme court of the territory of Washington."

And now, just a few words in closing. These sketches could have been much longer, but I had a certain sympathy for those who were to read them and hence have left out much that was vitally interesting to the writer at any rate. They have made up simply a bird's eye view of that wonderful period in the life of a pioneer.

They have brought to me kind expressions from many people I did not know, in that these good folk have assured me that the sketches were readable and of real value from the historic setting in which they were written. They have put me in closer personal touch with that army of our citizens who are numbered among those who had me for their teacher in an early day. They have made me acquainted with several descendants of my Iowa pupils who have migrated to this goodly land where they might make homes for their families.

I want one and all to know how much I appreciate this opportunity to present these sketches for your perusal and to assure you that this is now one of the chief joys of my long life. Most people wait until they have been called hence to have real appreciation shown them. I have been permitted to get my flowers when I can still enjoy their fragrance ere I pass into the "great beyond."

I want also to express to The Spokesman-Review and others who have made my connection with the paper so pleasant my hearty thanks. In the language of Father Eells:

"I shall hold them in grateful remembrance."

As a concluding word, may I say to the young people who read these articles:

"Plan for more than you can do;
    "Then do it.
"Bite off more than you can chew;
    "Then chew it.
"Hitch your wagon to a star;
    "Keep your seat and there you are."

Beginning Second Series

CHAPTER XII

TERRITORIAL BOARD OF EDUCATION

In November, 1881, I received a letter from Horace Stratton, a member of the upper house of our territorial assembly from Whitman county, written at Olympia, stating that he had recommended me to Governor William A. Newell as a suitable person to represent Eastern Washington upon the board of education. At that time the board consisted of four persons, including the territorial superintendent of schools, who was appointed by the governor and ratified by the upper house of the legislature.

In a fews days my commission arrived and was duly accepted. It is interesting in this connection to note that in pioneer days the honor of such an appointment was considered sufficient recompense for services rendered. Traveling expenses and hotel bills were paid by the territory. Can you imagine in this commercial age a body of educators, or for that matter, any other body, accepting an appointment under similar terms?

C. W. Wheeler of Waitsburg, ex-teacher and editor of the Waitsburg Times, was appointed superintendent of schools. R. C. Kerr of Port Townsend, the head of the schools in that city, represented Northwest Washington, while Mrs. P. C. Hale, a noted primary educator of Olympia, was called from Southwest Washington. Whatever may be said of our mentality, we were a weighty body in avoirdupois, for we turned the scale at more than 800 pounds.

Under the law, our meetings must be held the first week in April of each year, with such other meetings as might be necessary upon call of the superintendent. Accordingly, in the spring of 1882 I made my first trip to Olympia. The Cascades were not then, as now, tunneled by three great lines of railroad. I had to go to Dayton by stage, thence over the newly constructed O. R. & N. to Portland, where I must spend the night, and the next morning take a boat to Kalama. Then I was taken by train to Tenino and thence by a stub train into the capital of our territory, Olympia, with its mud flats and its Swantown which is now only a memory.

Two things which forcibly impressed me were the magnificent forests through which I passed after leaving Kalama and the unsightly mud flats. At the time of day when I arrived the tide was out and the town presented anything but a charming appearance.

The town at this date had possibly 2000 people. I could not but wonder why, with such a vast expanse of land as the territory of Washington possessed, so unsightly a place should have been selected for the capital city of what was to be a great state. Even then I had a vision of what was to come to pass ere many years elapsed. I have become reconciled to the inevitable and yet I feel still that Yakima or Ellensburg would have been a better site for our state capital.

I found a good hotel in the Carleton, where I was comfortably housed and became acquainted with the immense chunks of bark which were used in the fireplaces of the hotel. I could hardly believe it possible that any tree could have bark of such thickness.

I shall not tire my readers with the tedious routine of the business of that first session of the board, but simply say that I found my fellow members agreeable and competent. I was elected secretary and you will find in the office of the state superintendent the records of that meeting. Mrs. P. C. Hale and I were appointed a committee to draft a course of study for the schools of the territory. Thus I had the honor of writing the first course of study ever printed for the territory of Washington. I wrote it and Mrs. Hale simply assented to my work.

One of the interesting features of the session to me was the fact that one Mr. Balch, a lame gentleman, took the examination for a teacher's certificate and we had a hard time putting him through. Yet I have always felt that it was not lack of knowledge but pure scare which prevented his passing with flying colors. At any rate the other members of the board found great enjoyment in tormenting me, as they expressed it, the only susceptible member of the board, because of my anxiety to see him through in good shape.

I shall not dwell upon the second meeting of the board in April, 1883, I had resigned my work in Colfax and had planned to return to Iowa in the summer. The reason for my failure to do so will be narrated in a sketch yet to come.

In the fall of that year it was deemed best to hold a second session of the board at the time the meeting of our territorial legislature. There were some important matters relative to school legislation which demanded attention. The text book question, certification of teachers, the granting of life diplomas and some other matters of vital importance to our schools were to be considered.

The town was full of solons and hence I was invited to become the guest of Mrs. Hale, who lived just beyond Swantown, to which I have already alluded. Our meetings were for the most part held in the evening at her residence. This necessitated the other members of the board making trips in the rain and mud to the place of meeting. After nightfall, this was no pleasant task.

One dark stormy night, Mr. Kerr and one Mr. Barnes, a book agent, were on their way to the place of meeting. They had neglected to carry the necessary lantern and as they stumbled along in the darkness Mr. Kerr lost his balance and fell, but not upon the ground. When he attempted to rise he was astride a cow which had decided to take her evening rest in the road. He presented a grotesque appearance when he arrived at the place of meeting which was near the scene of his mishap.

By the way, speaking of the ubiquitous text book agent, they were abroad in the land at this particular time for the coming summer the territory was to vote upon new books for the ensuing five years. One of them found me out on the boat from Portland to Kalama en route to the capital. Nothing was too good for me. I must dine with him. He would send me a complete set of their best school books.

Some days after our arrival in Olympia he took occasion to remark:

"You know, Miss West, we have a superior set of books and you are in a position to be of great assistance to me in putting them over."

I looked at him and answered:

"Do you mean to imply, Mr.————(not Barnes), that you think I am open to a bribe? If so, let me say that you have entirely misjudged my character. Should the governor reappoint me upon the board, I shall give your books the same consideration that I do the others and the best books for our purpose will receive my vote."

BOARD OF EDUCATION

It is interesting to note that I ceased to receive his attention. When the appointments were made some time later I was left off of the board. You are at liberty to draw your own conclusions.

Some years later when the question of text books came up, a certain member of the board at the time admitted that he had been reimbursed to the tune of $2,000 for his vote to secure the adoption of a certain set of books.

The week proved to be a busy one for me for many sections of the school law were to be revised. As secretary of the board, I did much of the clerical work connected with the proposed changes. Among other things, it was my privilege to write entirely the first law granting life diplomas to teachers after 10 years' teaching experience, three years of which must have been in the territory of Washington.

Ere the adjournment of the assembly the governor had appointed R. C. Kerr superintendent of public instruction and my old pupil, John C. Lawrence, a member of the board. As it was my privilege to grant him his first certificate to teach in Washington, so it was his privilege to grant me my first territorial life diploma under the terms of the law which I had written for enactment by the legislative body.

Virtually the same thing is true relative to Josephine Corliss, now Mrs. Preston, state superintendent of public instruction. Her first certificate to teach in Washington was granted by me. Later she was my primary teacher in the Baker school. Still later I served for many years on the state board of teachers' examiners under her. Such are the queer quirks of fate!

I want to call special attention to the cut illustrating this article. The picture of the old territorial state house was taken when our first state governor, Elisha P. Ferry, was inaugurated. So far as is known, there are only two of these pictures in existence. One of them is in the possession of Mr. Hitt, state librarian, while the other belongs to J. C. Lawrence, who has loaned it to me for this sketch.

An effort is being made to have it placed, or rather have it reproduced, upon the entrance doors of our new state capitol building. Mr. Hitt tells me that the artist attempted to sell him the negative and before he had decided about taking it, it was burned.

My friends may be interested to know that several weeks ago when I visited in Olympia, I had an interview with Governor Hartley and was invited to lunch with him at the executive mansion.

When I said to him, "Governor Hartley, in the main, I agree with your policies but you are not 'as wise as a serpent and as harmless as a dove' in putting them over. In other words, you are too pugilistic!"

He smiled sweetly, sent for his chauffeur and sent me down town in his private car.

The Olympia of today is quite different from the Olympia of 40 years ago. The paved streets, the filled-in mud flats, the obliterated Swantown, the fine public and business houses, the excellent hotels and the beautiful homes make it in many respects a pleasant abiding place, even though it is quiet except during the sessions of the legislature.

The old Carlton hotel still stands, but has degenerated into a second-rate boarding house. There are few landmarks to recall the old-time town as I first knew it in 1882. Change, and change for the better, is written everywhere.

CHAPTER XIII

EXAMINATIONS AND INSTITUTES

From time immemorial the teachers' examination has been the chief bugbear which has confronted the real teacher and the would-be teacher as well. We have come to the time, however, when this is virtually removed. He who would teach must take a course of training in preparation for his work, just as the doctor, the lawyer or any other professional man must prepare for the work he expects to do in the world. This is as it should be.

Yet we haven't gone far enough. Some systems should be devised whereby those who can never become real teachers can be weeded out before they try out their lack of skill upon unfortunate children who are placed under their care. I have ideas along this line, but this is not the place for them. Hence I forbear.

Had you, my readers, been as I have, a teachers' examiner for more than a quarter of a century, you

EXAMINATIONS

would feel as I do the absurdity of the so-called teachers' examination. It has always been little less than a farce. Many of those who would have made the best teachers have failed, while many others, with what we call in this day "gall," have come through with flying colors.

Identically the same condition exists in our grade school examinations. A case in point: Forty-three years ago, when I began my school work in Walla Walla I was given a class in arithmetic of about 25 children. Perhaps half of the class were not qualified to go on with the work. In my wisdom, as I supposed, I decided to give them an examination and weed out those who ought to take the work over again.

Much to my distress, Julia Wertheimer, the best pupil in the class, failed miserably. She was so frightened for fear of failure that she was unable to answer the simplest questions. The ignorant ones, in some cases, obtained passing grades. I did the only thing possible, put the papers in the fire and announced that I had changed my mind and all could go on to the end of the term.

An examination can at best give only a partial knowledge of the scholastic attainments of the prospective teacher. This is only one of the many important qualifications of one who would successfully lead the young in securing an education. Here again I must pause, as the qualifications of the teacher is not my subject.

THE WIDE NORTHWEST

For about a dozen years I have been a member of the state board of teachers' examiners. Before I take up the subject of institutes, I want to give you two or three interesting answers to questions in physiology. That was my main subject in grading papers:

Question—Describe the lymphatic system.

Answer—The lymphatic system is one which begins nowhere and ends anywhere.

Question—Why drink much water every day?

Answer—Inasmuch as three-fourths of the weight of the body is water, therefore, we should drink that much water every day.

Imagine me, with my 200 pounds avoirdupois, drinking 150 pounds of water daily!

Question—What are the uses of pain?

Answer—To make us feel uncomfortable.

I could write volumes of ridiculous answers to questions any school child should answer intelligently. I rejoice in the fact that we are to have little more of this kind of foolishness and that a saner way of noting the qualifications of teachers scholastically is to be adopted.

Would that there might also be a way devised of testing out teachers as to their other qualifications, which to my mind are of vastly greater importance than their book knowledge. I do not underrate that in the smallest particular.

EXAMINATIONS

Fifty-eight years ago, when I began my teaching career, we were dependent upon the public and private schools for whatever pedagogical knowledge we might acquire, except for the teachers' institutes. They had already found a place in many sections of the country. They were then devoted more to instruction in methods and not so much as advertising mediums for schools in the sections where they were held.

I think it was in 1871 that I first heard of a normal school in New York state and a year or so later of another at Plattville, Wis. It was in 1876 before the first normal school was established in Iowa and about the same time that the San Jose normal made its debut in California.

The last-named was presided over, in the first place, by President Allen, a man of wonderful personality, who inspired his student body with a desire in each case to be a second Professor Allen. This was impossible. In consequence, the graduates from the institution were for some years handicapped in the successful prosecution of their work for there could only be one President Allen.

Because of this fact, few people on the Coast, when I first arrived, wanted the normal graduates in their employ. All that has long since passed and we are flying to the opposite extreme and are coming to imagine that normal training is absolutely needful for successful teaching.

115

THE WIDE NORTHWEST

The first teachers' institute was held in Walla Walla in 1883 with J. H. Morgan as superintendent of the county schools. I was elected secretary of that body and continued to serve for eighteen years. When I left the county in 1901, Miss Mamie Thomas was elected secretary. If I am not mistaken, she has served ever since without a break.

Miss Thomas was for some years my assistant in the Baker school in Walla Walla. She has been for a long time principal of the Sharpstein school in Walla Walla. I feel impelled to tell a story of Mr. Morgan's last institute which illustrates so forcibly the things we remember and the things we forget.

Some ten years ago I had occasion to call upon a lady here in Spokane on a matter of business. When I was ushered into her room, I met another woman of perhaps 50. When introduced, she said to me:

"I have never met you before, Miss West, but I have never forgotten you."

Naturally I was curious and asked how that could be.

"It was something you said at Mr. Morgan's last institute in Walla Walla. It made a profound impression upon me and I have never forgotten it."

Then I was pleased because I remembered having read a paper upon the teaching of language in our public schools, rather than technical grammar. I thought surely that was worth while. But when I spoke of the paper she said:

116

EXAMINATIONS

"No, that wasn't it. It was what you said in answer to roll call."

Then it came back to me. After I had concluded calling the roll at one session and the teachers present had responded with a familiar quotation, Mr. Morgan called my name and I was expected to respond in the same fashion. That last afternoon I rose in response to my name and said:

> "Man wants but little here below,
> Nor wants that little long."

Then I added:

"I have often wondered if that is the reason nobody ever wanted me."

Of course the people laughed and Mr. Morgan whispered:

"How did you think of it? I wouldn't have thought of it in a hundred years and if I had thought of it I wouldn't have said it for a hundred dollars."

Now, I submit that this was worth while. That woman remembered, just as we would, the foolish thing and forgot all about what was really of some value.

The public generally took a much greater interest in these gatherings than they have of late years for the simple reason that more attention was given to matters of vital interest to teachers and the public generally. Of late years institutes have come to be simply advertising mediums, or the exploiting of some pet foible, such as anti-vivisection and the like. I remember some 30 years ago a certain gentleman from one of the rural districts who rose one morning and spoke at considerable length upon the cruelty taught children by the vivisectionist.

At the noon hour somebody placed upon my desk a letter sealed and addressed to the gentleman in question. When he opened the letter he found a big, fat bedbug. You know, or can imagine, the rest.

Our evening sessions were usually largely attended and we had often some fine lectures. I remember one night in the brick church (Presbyterian) when I was sandwiched in between the Rev. Ezra Haskell of the Congregational Church and Dr. Lathrope of the Episcopal. How proud I felt when the Rev. T. M. Gunn, who had just arrived from Joliet, Ill., to take charge of the brick congregation, came across the church, requested an introduction and asked if he might have a copy of my paper to send to his home town where he wanted to have it published!

Mr. Gunn sent two children to school to me after that and so far as I know he never had occasion to regret his having given me that little boost in his home town. I am appending herewith the lines which were published in the Joliet Daily News, November, 1885, with a delightful footnote telling of the way we did things on the Pacific Coast. The poem follows:

EXAMINATIONS

What work is more noble, what work is more grand
Than leading up higher the young of the land;
Than helping the boys and girls on the way
As with slow but sure footsteps they climb day by day;
Than guiding them ever with patience and care,
As they earnestly seek for gems rich and rare?
For this service so high and so full of delight,
Many true hearts have enlisted and do with their
    might
What their hands find to do, and yet I am sure
There are many whose work can never endure
When tried by the test of that infinite love
Which prompts one to build for the mansions above.

*   *   *

Very many of those who are trying to teach,
Simply do so because they much want to reach
Some goal in the future, and this end to attain,
They are teaching our schools a few dollars to gain.
A girl wants to marry; she has no money to buy
The finery she needs; she therefore must try
To earn it in some way, why not take a school?
She can teach very cheap and the wise men who rule
In the choice of instructors are often quite kind,
And cheap teachers are what they are anxious to find,
A young man wants money, and he too decides
That he'll take a school, though he frankly confides
In his friends and assures them that he
Has no love for the work, but he is striving to be
A professional man and his studies demand
An income much greater than he has at hand.

THE WIDE NORTHWEST

The schools are obtained but you can believe
That districts, in such cases, value receive
For the money they pay. Three chances to one
'Twill be found at the close when the term's work is
    done;
The contracts are ended; the money is paid;
That the children instructed no advancement have
    made.

               ★   ★   ★

The work has vexations and I'm frank to admit
There are times when all teachers are ready to quit,
And yet, after all, I really believe
That every true teacher does surely receive
The peace and the joy that comes to that one
Who feels that in life his work is well done.
Fellow teachers rejoice, be earnest, be strong,
Though the trials may be many it will not be long
Till the clouds break away and the sun shining
    through
Shall bring in great measure choice blessings to you.
For the great master teacher who dwelleth above
Is guiding us ever with tenderest love.

L. L. WEST.
Walla Walla, W. T., Nov. 1885.

CHAPTER XIV

BEGINNING WALLA WALLA WORK IN BAKER SCHOOL

Just prior to my leaving Whitman county in March, 1883, Judge Caton of Walla Walla attended a court session in Colfax. When I met him one day he said to me:

"Miss West, I wish you could see your way clear to join our Walla Walla force of teachers."

I laughed and told him I expected to go to California immediately after the meeting of the territorial board of education and from there back to Iowa to take up the work I left when I came to Washington.

However, "man proposes but God disposes." The Rev. D. J. Pierce, a member of our Colfax board of trustees, had invited me to spend a couple of nights in his Walla Walla home, en route to Olympia. The next morning after my arrival he took me to see the Baker

121

school building just being completed, then the finest school building in Washington territory. He said:

"I want you to meet F. W. Paine, the president of the school board." We called at his office, but found him out.

May I digress here to say that in all my life I have never known a more capable school official than Mr. Paine. I was highly indignant when, some time after my leaving Walla Walla, I learned that, because of political animus, the school which had been named for him had by a new school board been changed to the Lincoln school.

On the next morning at 5 o'clock, I left for Portland, telling Mr. Pierce I expected to stop at the Esmond hotel. I found on the train a friend from Colfax, who suggested that I would find the St. Charles a better place to stop. I accordingly went there.

On Sunday evening, soon after I reached Olympia, Mr. Wheeler arrived and the first thing he said to me was:

"I see you are going to Walla Walla to take a position in the schools there."

I laughed and remarked that it was news to me but he assured me he had read it in two Walla Walla papers. Still I wasn't interested.

On Wednesday a boy came to the office where we worked from the postmaster with a letter. He asked if Miss West was present, stating that the letter was marked "important" and had arrived Saturday at his office, and had not been called for. It proved to be from Mr. Pierce. He stated that a couple of hours after I left his home, Judge Sharpstein, another member of the school board, had called and asked for me, stating that he had been informed I was leaving Colfax.

They wanted to secure my services if possible. The judge had telegraphed the Esmond but received no reply. I need not enter into further particulars. This explains why I did not return to Iowa as I had planned. It simply meant that I was to accept a position in the Baker school. There I was to remain for more than 18 years, most of the time as principal.

May I add, I should likely have been there still had it not been for politics? In the spring of 1901, when a "political boss" made his appearance on the stage of action, he sent me word that I might have my position still if I desired it. I declined with thanks. I have never stayed anywhere except on merit.

I have been asked why the school was called the Baker. Simply because Dr. Baker, father of the first railroad into the city, gave a block of ground for school purposes upon which to erect the school building. It was the nucleus of the present school system of the city which now has several fine buildings and last year had 122 teachers.

I want to add here that in my 54 years of service

I filled but one position as a teacher for which I applied, except in the sense that each year I let the board know that I would accept the position if they desired to retain my services. I wonder how many teachers can beat that record?

I found the Baker school upon my arrival in the city with five teachers. I made the sixth. The Park street school had two teachers and the Eighth street school also had two teachers. These schools were each running an independent line, although just prior to my coming Professor Brock, the country superintendent of schools, had been made superintendent of the city schools as well.

Right here, there is another interesting thing I want to record. Mr. Brock was paid $80 a month, while Miss Tina Johnston, as principal of the Baker school, and I, as assistant principal, were paid identically the same salary, viz., $80 a month. That was big pay in those days.

I want also to state that my salary was raised three times during my stay in Walla Walla and always without solicitation on my part. Again, during the first six years of my work there, my pay was always received in $20 gold pieces, except that after the first year, when my salary was raised first to $85, then to $95 and then to $100, the odd amounts were in smaller gold.

When several years after my arrival, I became principal, the salary of the assistant was reduced to $65 a month. When the friends of the incumbent went to the board, remonstrating, the answer given was "Miss West is a special teacher and hence is entitled to more than an ordinary teacher." This was fine for me, but not so fine for the other fellow.

Almost immediately after my arrival I took up the matter of a regular course of study for the schools.

This was of special importance, because, as already stated, the territory had as yet no printed course of study for the schools. This was printed in the winter of 1883-84.

The school board appointed Superintendent Brock, Miss Johnston and myself as the committee to draft the needed course of study. As secretary of the committee, I had the honor of writing the manuscript, my work being assented to by the other members. This was adopted by the board and so we became a regularly organized graded school, the second, if I mistake not, in the territory. The Denny school in Seattle, was the other one.

Until just recently, when Professor Jones, who was the principal of the Denny school at that date, passed to his reward, we ranked as the oldest teachers in point of service in the state.

May I say in passing that Professor Jones was in many respects a great man? His memory and influence on the young people of the Sound country of that period will never die.

During the first two years of my service in Walla Walla, there is little of interest to record except that in the summer of 1884 Professor Frank Rigler, who later made name and fame for himself in Portland, Oregon, came to become principal of the schools, supplanting Professor Brock. Mr. Rigler was a real educator.

The one incident connected with his residence in Walla Walla that I want to record is that there entered my class that fall a bright, attractive young lady of 16 who told me when I asked her for her name that it was "Babe Koehler." I responded:

"Why, child, that is not a suitable name for a young woman."

She assured me that it was all she had. Six weeks later, she came to me one day and said: "Will you please change my name to 'Leni Leoti'?"

I laughed, and she told me that she liked my name and had decided to make it her own. A year later she married Mr. Rigler, and, since his death, she has married again and now lives in Portland with her second husband.

On December 19, 1884, it began to snow and kept it up for a full three days when the snow at Walla Walla was three feet deep on the level. At The Dalles, Ore., it was 11 feet in depth. Two O. R. & N. trains were stalled not far from that point and for three weeks, the passengers were fed by the railroad company. Two conductors, one Mr. Barnes, and the other, if I remember correctly, Mr. Lyons, made names for themselves in caring for the comfort of the stalled passengers.

That winter we had decided to have a great union Christmas tree for all the Sunday schools of the city at Small's opera house. It seated comfortably 1200 people. Committees were appointed. Literally tons of Christmas presents of candy, nuts, toys and all the other things which go with such festive occasions were brought to the building. At 6 o'clock, the work was completed and all went to their homes for supper, excepting a man and his wife who were left as caretakers.

A half hour later, the roof, because of the weight of accumulated snow and ice, collapsed, and the room was filled with debris. Fortunately, the peolpe were near the beautiful trees fully laden with the presents, and so no one was injured. Had the accident occurred an hour later, many people would have been wiped out of existence.

I have never before or since experienced a period when all hearts were filled with such a spirit of thankfulness as then. I am one of those who believe that the great "I am," who controls the destinies of the human family, protects each individual born into the world until such time as his work is accomplished.

Henry Rasmus, who later became one of the great Methodist preachers of his day and at one time pastor of the now Central Methodist church in Spokane, was a member of that company of people. He was then a blacksmith and the only promise he gave of his future greatness was the fact that we were members of the same literary society where he delighted to appear upon the program on every possible occasion.

If I am not mistaken, his ambition then was to be an actor. I am inclined to believe that the coming of "Camp Meeting Johnny" Naugle, a distinguished evangelist from the middle west, to hold a series of revival meetings changed his plans. He became a great preacher instead. I heard Dr. Rasmus allude to the incident just narrated in a sermon he preached in Spokane last June.

The presents were reclaimed from the wrecked building on Christmas day. Everybody was happy.

I want to call attention to Miss Mary J. Thomas, who has had a continued teaching service in Walla Walla for 43 years. She was young when she began her work there. She is looked upon as one of the strong teachers of the state, and probably the oldest from point of continued service at the same school in the state.

It is interesting to note that at this time there were five teachers in the Walla Walla schools, including Miss Thomas, who were there when I left the town 25 years ago. Three of them are old pupils of mine and another that I tutored for her first grade certificate. Who says I didn't leave an impress upon the public school system of Walla Walla county?

WORK IN WALLA WALLA

A quarter of a century ago, 60 per cent of all the teachers in the county were my old pupils, besides many who were teaching elsewhere.

When I began my work in Walla Walla, it had a population of about 2,500 people. For some years its growth was slow. In spite of its beautiful situation and, at most seasons of the year, delightful climate, it was not easy of access. This retarded its growth for a long time.

I am frank to confess that I have never in my life seen a more beautiful place, especially during the months of May and June of each year. The soft, balmy air, the beautiful flowers and trees, the well-kept lawns, the fine homes and business houses, the graded streets, the wonderful college spirit (loyalty to Whitman), and above all, the kindly, gracious people make it a place much to be desired as a home town.

On December 12, 1886, I wrote and had published in the Sunday Journal the following picture of the growth of the town, which I am going to include, as it illustrates not simply the town of Walla Walla, but all this great Inland Empire. I made no mistake in my prophecy of what was to be.

A Picture

As the darkness of night now filling my room
So the future before me lies shrouded in gloom;
But a hand draws the curtain and full on my sight
A picture appears, resplendent and bright.

THE WIDE NORTHWEST

In panoramic array the years are unrolled
Till at last the year nineteen hundred is told.
In the picture, our country, the Pacific domain
I see, freed forever from tyranny's reign.
Corporations no longer with despotic power
Wrest from our freemen the God-given dower.
The hillsides and valleys now blossom to bring
Gold to their owners, and glad children sing
A song of rejoicing. The lands, now well tilled,
Yield the joy and the blessings of garners well-filled.
The railroads, deposed, now traverse the land
And as good public servants each lend helping hand.
In the grand onward march of our noble young state,
Already becoming both wealthy and great,
The east and the west united at last,
Are helping each other forgetting the past.
In our broad eastern empire, I see everywhere
Signs of advancement; the towns, here and there
All show rapid growth, but the city still queen
Is the town of two Wallas on whose streets are seen
Much business thrift. The city has grown—
Population, ten thousand. Its people are known
As a people who hold their city's good name
Of greater importance than riches or fame.
The beer halls and gin shops no longer disgrace
The streets of the city, but filling their place,
Are tall wholesale houses, through whose open doors
Are passing supplies to fill other stores.
The churches have grown. The newspapers stand
Among the first dailies of our favored land.
The faces and names now familiar they seem!

WORK IN WALLA WALLA

I can hardly believe it is only a dream.
This beautiful picture—could I but portray
One-half of its beauties I'm sure you would say
'Tis a God-given country and the Father hath led
And guided us onward, as Israel was fed.
But slowly the vision is fading away
And I am brought back to the scenes of today
With its bustle, its turmoil, its unceasing strife,
With the trials and the troubles belonging to life.
Permit me to add, of this one thing I'm sure—
The work now being done will always endure;
And the years will be few till proud Washington state
Becomes populous and rich—'tis as certain as fate.

December 12, 1886.

CHAPTER XV

ORGANIZING THE HIGH SCHOOL

When the question of the high school was first suggested, a good deal of bitter opposition was aroused. Many people felt that the education of children at public expense should end with the grammar grades. But just as "a continual dripping of water wears away the stone," so, in time, enough people came to our way of thinking to permit the organization of the school.

You will still find many who object strenuously to the so-called "higher education" for the masses of the people. However, it isn't my province to discuss this controversial point but to deal with facts as to the organization of our school.

In 1889 we started the school in the old Baker building and taught a ninth grade class that first year. Superintendent Kerr and I did the work in connection with our other classes. The school board decided to complete the third floor of the Paine building for high school purposes.

ORGANIZING HIGH SCHOOL

The school, accordingly, moved in the fall of 1890 into its new quarters. Mr. Kerr went with it as principal in connection with his work as superintendent of the city schools. He urged me to go with him as assistant because he recognized his weakness as a disciplinarian. He knew I was strong in this particular.

I didn't want to go, and told him so. I finally went to Mr. Paine and told him I was willing to do whatever he thought best. His response when I said that I preferred to stay in the Baker school was:

"I should think you would."

That settled it, but when I told Mr. Kerr of the interview, he shook his head and said:

"I do not think it wise, Miss West, but if Paine says so, it will have to go. You know that women are infernally mean to other women, so you are likely to have trouble here."

The after events in no sense justified his prediction. Of course, there is sometimes disloyalty among women, but no more so than among men. I left the Baker school many years later with a record of having the best-governed school in the city. Everything moved like clockwork. I never had any serious difficulty with the teachers.

Twenty-five years after I began teaching in Walla Walla I went back to the city to speak at an institute. While in town Josephine Paine gave me a reception at their home. Mr. Paine came before I left, bringing me a beautiful bunch of carnations. When I expressed my appreciation of the delightful things being done for me, he said:

"We ought to show you appreciation, for everybody knows that you and Professor Kerr made our public schools."

That was a compliment worth while.

Miss Lillian Blair was selected as the first assistant in the new high school. She was a fine young woman, but she was lacking in that particular which is so essential to successful teaching, or, in fact, to any line of human endeavor. She was not a disciplinarian and so was unable to supplement the work of her principal, who, as I have already stated, was weak in this particular.

May I say just here that Professor Kerr stayed with the school until 1901, when he was "let out" because of political and religious influences which came to permeate the board? These two things are not good bed-fellows and well-nigh wrecked the schools for a time.

The trouble was overcome after a time. Today Walla Walla has a fine school system, well manned and with magnificent buildings for the work.

Miss Blair was followed by Miss Richards, who stayed a couple of years. Then came Miss Rose Dovell, who was with the school for a period of years and gave excellent satisfaction. She is now Mrs. Judge Lyons of Seattle.

But going back to Professor Kerr: He was the most scholarly man I ever knew—a man of fine presence, but with a bad temper well disciplined. Yet he could not discipline others. He was unfortunate in that he had just a "nubbin" of a nose. I have heard him say many times that if it were not for his nose, he would have been president of the United States. It is noteworthy that all our great men and women were people with large, well-developed noses.

When, in the spring of 1901, it became evident that he would likely be "let out," I begged him again and again to resign and not give his enemies a chance to drop him. He wouldn't do it. When the blow came, it all but crushed this truly good man. He continued his work until the end of the year and then left the city with the avowed purpose of never entering its doors again. He passed to his reward something more than a year ago.

As I have said, his chief lack was discipline. I want here to enter my earnest protest against the present lack of discipline in our schools and elsewhere. It is undoubtedly the greatest defect of our school system today. Children who are not properly controlled in their homes and in the lower grades are correspondingly harder to control as they advance in years.

This condition, as I see it, is largely due to the present departmental system, so popular and in vogue in many of our schools. It is without question important that children should receive instruction from experts, as far as possible, in all branches of secular education, but it is vitally more important that their teachers should come to know them better in order that they might encourage or restrain, wherever needful, the children placed under their care.

This can never be accomplished where the teacher has the child but a single period of from 30 to 45 minutes daily. It is the close personal contact that counts. The study hall periods are not the same, and then, too, the teachers should come to know more intimately the parents of their pupils if they hope to secure the best results.

My readers may think me a crank but I really know what I am talking about. My most satisfactory work has always been with those children who have been under my personal supervision for a year or longer.

May I in this connection relate a most delightful experience with the Walla Walla high school which must ever be dear to my heart? About six years ago I was in the city. Going to the principal at the time, Professor Jones, I told him I should like the privilege of speaking to his student body.

To this he consented, saying that we would spend the hour until 10 o'clock in visiting the various rooms that I might come to know their system of self-government which was then in use. I found this to be working admirably and when the hour arrived, I stood in their fine auditorium before an audience of 1,000 boys and girls with their teachers and spoke for 45 minutes.

They encored me and I spoke for 15 minutes longer. At this point, Mr. Jones called to the platform young Augustavo, whose father had been a pupil of mine, and this sturdy auburn-haired youth led them in their school yells. Then after the singing of their school songs the principal said:

"Now, all of Miss West's grandchildren, who desire may come on the platform and shake hands with her."

In response 75 young people came forward and taking me by the hand told me who their fathers and mothers were. In many cases I had taught both parents.

These were followed by perhaps 25 more who said that while their parents did not go to school to me, they wanted to shake hands anyhow. Mr. Jones said:

"After this exhibition, it pays to be a teacher if you never make a dollar out of it:"

I think it was in 1902 that we graduated the first class from the high school. Some of them entered the work of teaching and have made names for themselves along this line, while others made good along other lines of work. In the years since, the wisdom of organizing the school has been fully demonstrated by the fine body of young people who have gone out from its doors to fill honored places in society and in the business world as well.

I was amused some years ago, just after Oscar Cain, now deceased, had purchased his fine home on Cook street, in Spokane, to have him say to me when I congratulated him on his purchase.

"Yes, Miss West, it is a fine home, but I feel a good deal like Bill Stine of Walla Walla after the erection of the high school building. As I went to my office each morning, I often found him out in front of his home looking at the school building and as I passed he said: 'A fine building, Oscar, if we could only afford it.' I feel a good deal the same way about my home."

CHAPTER XVI.

THE COLUMBIAN EXPOSITION. BOYS WHO BECAME MINISTERS

Walla Walla in pioneer days put over several celebrations of considerable interest. The first of these occurred on September 8, 1883. It was in honor of Henry Villard, who visited the town upon the completion of the Northern Pacific railroad.

Two things fix the date forcefully in my memory. We had our first rain after a long dry spell which had lasted from May 19th to the time indicated. The great arch was made entirely of wheat sacks which had been erected upon our lower Main street. This was to show the honorable gentleman our great need of better transportation to the sea and the markets of the world.

But easily the most notable event of pioneer times was the 400th anniversary celebration in 1892 of the landing of Christopher Columbus upon the shores of the new world. This was the more remarkable because a centennial celebration can only occur once in the lifetime of three generations of the human family. There seem to have been a good many such gatherings in different sections of the United States. So far as I know, Walla Walla was the only place in Washington where such a celebration was held.

A suggested program of exercises had been sent out from New York city. About the time of the opening of our fall term of school Mayor John L. Roberts sent out a call for the people to come together to arrange for the event.

Professor Kerr was selected from the high school and I from the grade schools to have places upon the committee. In just a day or two, we met upon call of J. L. Roberts, our chairman, to plan for the affair.

It was determined that all the children of the city and adjoining country districts, who desired to enter for the parade, should be drilled and be provided with banners and such other paraphernalia as might be deemed desirable. On the morning of the day designated they were to come to the Baker school where they were to form in line and then march to meet the other parts of the monster parade which had been planned.

From this point the children with their teachers were to march to the Paine school, a mile away. There the celebration was to be held. A platform had been erected in the open for the purpose. This was no small undertaking but everybody had a mind to work and it was accomplished.

Because I had the children from the military reservation in my school and so had an acquaintance with the officials of the fort, I was selected to see the commanding officer and ask for his assistance with the band and in any other way that he might be able to give. I shall not soon forget the gracious reception I received or how pleased I was when he said:

"Certainly, Miss West, I shall be only too glad to help you in your undertaking. The band will be provided and I shall order out a detachment of mounted soldiers to march in the parade. In the afternoon we will furnish you a sham battle to be fought on the fairgrounds."

Perhaps you think I wasn't proud to convey to the committee the results of my interview. I want to say in this connection that upon a number of occasions I called upon the fort for help and they never once turned me down. In return, I saw to it that their children received the best possible instruction in our school. They were fully appreciative of this fact.

When I read the printed program I discovered that it called for a high school boy to commit to memory an oration and deliver it to the audience. As I read the oration I knew that there was just one boy in the schools who could do this in a specially creditable manner. He was then in the eighth grade.

THE WIDE NORTHWEST

When I suggested Timothy Paul for the part, a storm of protest was aroused. It took some diplomacy and a lot of argument to convince the other members of the committee that I was right. I carried my point and to Tim went the honor. Both he and his people were profoundly grateful to me. I had the added satisfaction of knowing that no mistake had been made in the selection, as was generally conceded.

Later Tim studied law, married Josephine Paine, another of my pupils, and today they with their family reside in Walla Walla. Tim is doing well in his profession.

Everything was ready and that fine October morning of 1892 we gathered at the Baker school as planned. Even the clerk of the weather was good to us. Recognizing the importance of the occasion, he gave us the finest day at his disposal.

It was a sight long to be remembered as these happy children, more than 1300 strong, who formed in lines with banners flying. Singing lustily patriotic songs, they marched to meet the rest of the parade and so on through the principal streets of the city to the Paine school where seats had been provided for them.

I shall not weary my readers with the events of the next hour, except to say that everything went off as planned. When at noon we dispersed, it was a happy, hungry crowd that hurried home for the midday meal and then made preparation for the battle of the afternoon.

Mr. Roberts had arranged for a lot of wagons, more than 30, to be brought into town. These were fastened together. They in turn were attached to a big traction engine which was to draw the children and their teachers to the fair-grounds. It was a novel sight, 30 or 40 children and a teacher being crowded into each wagon. Then at 2 o'clock, the signal was given and we were off.

This was my first automobile ride. It was slow, to be sure, but we moved ahead until we were almost there when the pesky machine took a notion not to go. After a number of fruitless efforts to start it, we tumbled out and made our way on foot to the place where we were to see the fight.

After a couple of hours when the fight was over and we were ready to return to the city, the engine still proved balky. We started to walk home, but Al Lowe, our veteran truck man, came along just then with his big truck, drawn by two immense horses. At his invitation, I got aboard with a lot of children and we rode back into the city in state. This was fully as enjoyable as the ride out and quite as novel.

I had hoped to secure a picture of the parade but have been unable to find one. In a letter recently received from Tim Paul, he says:

"If you can use the enclosed photograph, I shall of course, be highly flattered and will be pleased if you will accept it from me as a reminder of the interesting times when you used to hold me on your lap before the rest of the school. I hold it against you, however, that once when I was sent to your room, I was grabbed by the collar and danced around pretty lively."

You notice he displays a forgiving spirit. I have had to make this article somewhat shorter than I expected, owing to the fact that some material I needed with which to refresh my memory is not available. In my next sketch I shall introduce some more of the more notable pupils of that Walla Walla period. A few are presented herewith.

Unlike my experience at Colfax, I can here boast of a number of ministers in the lot. Perhaps I had grown better or more exemplary in my conduct and so everted a greater influence for good upon the pupils! At any rate, I have to report a number of the boys who have become more or less distinguished along this line of endeavor.

Shall we begin with Harry Painter? I remember well how his eyes used to shine and how he wriggled in his seat when I asked the advanced class a question in history and no one seemed to be able to answer it, until I said:

"Well, Harry, you will have to tell them the answer."

Harry is now pastor of the Congregational church at Cheney, where it would seem he holds a life job.

He is moderator of their association and has held the position of grand chaplain in the Masonic lodge for many years.

The Rev. B. E. Koontz is pastor of the Methodist Episcopal church at Pasco. He has held many official positions in his church councils and is most highly regarded as an eloquent, conscientious preacher of the word.

The Rev. Harry Wintler, when last heard from, was serving a Presbyterian church in one of the large suburbs of Oakland, Calif.

I can still see him as he used to come to school in the early morning with his hands full of beautiful roses for his teacher. His mother was a good deal of a florist. I never lacked for flowers while he attended my school.

But I must not forget David Graham. He came to the city with his father from Arkansas. When he was in my classes he was distinguished largely because, while he nearly always had a good lesson, he found it necessary to add a little something of his own ideas along the line of the subject under consideration and so was often marked down.

Later, he graduated from Whitman College and is now a missionary of the Baptist church in China. You will note that I didn't confine my work to Baptist teaching alone. Here are four great denominations represented.

CHAPTER XVII

SOME NOTABLE MEN AND WOMEN

I can appreciate the pride some parents feel when their boys and girls distinguish themselves in their chosen life work. I know the pleasure I feel in the success of those whom I have helped in acquiring the rudiments of a secular training, needful for the successful prosecution of any line of human endeavor. It is that universal parenthood which fills my heart for every boy and girl it has been my privilege to teach. It is a joy to meet them, to clasp hands, look into their eyes and realize that they have made good, or perhaps, to experience a feeling of regret when I know that they have fallen by the wayside.

So I find much real pleasure in recording the names of some and telling just a little of the success which has attended their endeavors as they battled with the world.

When I went into that magnificent bookbinding and printing establishment (the Pioneer) in Tacoma and realized that this was owned and run by my boys, Alvah, Mort and Bill Howe, who, with their sisters, one of whom, Emma, went to school to me in the old Baker, I really felt that in a sense I had a part interest in the affair. Alvah is said to be a fine executive. Following in the footsteps of his mother, he has made the institution a real power in the city. Mort is head of a branch house in Chicago, while Emma, now Mrs. Perry Lyons, resides in Seattle where she has recognition as one of the prominent florists of that city.

Alex Cole, whom you all know as the head of a big printing house in "Sunny Old Spokane," is doing real credit to his family. I was puffed up with pride when I heard him say one time that I was the only real teacher he ever had.

James E. Duff of The Spokesman-Review was one of my boys of whom I am proud. He had the good judgment when he grew to manhood to select one of my choice girls, Myrtle Gardner, as his wife.

Frederic L. Earp, who materially assisted E. S. Evans and Linton Wells of Detroit in their 1926 round-the-world record trip by arranging their itinerary from quarantine at Victoria, B. C., to Sandpoint, near Seattle, is another of the boys. He began his newspaper work on the Walla Walla Union, served in the World war, has been a syndicate writer, an arctic explorer and is now in the employ of a Seattle newspaper.

By the way, speaking of the Union, another of the boys, John McDonald, after he secured his education, practiced law for a time and then took editorial charge of the paper, serving in that capacity until his death just a few months ago. John had two sisters, both of whom were old pupils. They later married, as all sensible young women should when they have the right kind of an opportunity.

Still another one of my boys, Edwin R. Collins, has made name and fame for himself as a newspaper man. From a boy, he delighted to write and was always ready with his English. He is small of stature and when the Spanish-American war was declared he wanted to go. He enlisted and went with the boys to Tacoma.

When he was weighed, he lacked one and one-half pounds of the requirement. This did not deter the young man. He went back to his quarters and drank water faithfully for 24 hours. Filling up with the liquid nourishment, he demanded a second test.

This time he weighed a fraction of a pound more than was necessary. He went with his company. Upon his return he was located for a time at Portland as city editor of an evening paper. While there, he was approached by a man from Boston who was out in the interests of Human Life, a monthly publication of the city of culture.

He stated that his paper was getting out an educational number and wanted to run a short biographical sketch of a representative teacher from each of six sections of the United States, together with their pictures. As a result of this interview, my picture appeared as the teacher from the northwest section of the country. It was an honor to be classed with Ella Flagg Young of Chicago and other educational leaders.

Ned is now managing editor of the Los Angeles Evening Herald, and editorial manager of all evening publications on the Pacific coast for an eastern publisher.

Miles and Dan Kyger, who went to the Philippines with Ned, passed to their reward while there. They were fine promising young men who were ready to give their lives in the cause of liberty for the oppressed. Their sister, Tot, married and still lives in Walla Walla.

One of the earlier pupils was Harvey Yenney, who has been for years a prosperous farmer. George Drumheller of a later date is recognized as the "wheat king of the Walla Walla valley." In a single year his check in payment for his crop has been $250,000, it is said. I notice by the papers that he has more recently turned his attention to the breeding of fine horses.

Ed Noack is now the head of a large manufacturing plant at Stockton, Calif. Louis Sutherland is associated with his father in business in Walla Walla. Ray, the older son, a boy of fine promise, died while quite young.

THE WIDE NORTHWEST

Dave Stokes, now ill, has been for many years a resident of Spokane. He is well known as a hardware man. Mrs. Stokes is prominent in club and musical work.

One morning just prior to the opening of school Mrs. Aeils, the wife of a grocer in the city, came bringing to me two twin boys, John and Dooley Middike, who had just arrived from Holland. They were about 8 years old and couldn't speak a word of English.

I took them to the primary department and they began work. Eight years later they graduated from the Baker school with honor. Today John is a prominent merchant of Seattle, while Dooley is doing a good insurance and real estate business in Everett.

Dorsey Hill, now treasurer of Whitman College, has the distinction of spending eight years in the Baker school and finishing his work there without being absent or tardy once. His sister, Bertha, is now Mrs. Bayless and resides in Los Angeles.

Ray Passage, now a business man of Seattle, has a wife and five children. When I was teaching at Camano he sent me a couple of boxes of fine oranges, marking them: "For you and the kiddies."

Harry Burford is a big insurance man in Los Angeles and is doing a fine business. His sister, Bess, married Charlie McKean and lives in Walla Walla.

Frank Lowdon, president of the Walla Walla Chamber of Commerce, has become a fine business man.

Howard Knott studied medicine and now one of the leading physicians and surgeons in Seattle. Charlie Denent, with whom he had a fight in the days when they were third grade boys, is a revenue collector for the government at Yakima.

When Miss Markham, their teacher, asked me what ought to be done with them, I said, after listening to their tales of woe:

"Well, boys, you can shake hands, kiss each other and make up, or kiss me."

Boys hate to kiss each other, but they decided to choose the lessor of two evils and so kissed as directed. They then passed out to the playgrounds and I stepped on the front porch just in time to hear Charlie say:

"Howard, I had rather kiss you 11 times than kiss Miss West once."

Hard on me, but it was effective so far as the boys were concerned.

Addie Denny of Waitsburg, when she started to school to me, had an ambition to be as tall as I. She attained her desire and then some. She later went to the San Jose normal school, became a successful teacher, married Albert Dickinson of her home town and later she became deputy state superintendent of public instruction under Mrs. Josephine Preston. She is still connected with the office for part time.

THE WIDE NORTHWEST

Nettie Galbraith has been for many years the head of St. Paul's school in Walla Walla, where she is spoken of as a really great teacher.

Rachel Hamilton taught, studied, made a trip to Europe to complete her education and is now one of the language professors in the state university in Seattle.

Stella Lacy, Rose Lucinger, Margaret McCausland and Blanche Kelling are still at work in the schoolroom.

Merton Brewer, who has been twice married, is a successful lawyer and business man of Auburn. His second wife is a charming woman. They have several fine children.

Al Kelling is located in Portland, Ore. Here also we find Ed McNeill, Harry Joy and Wilbur Fiske Brock, who was for many years a newspaper man and is now a farmer, and Charles Dutcher, who holds an important government position.

While in Portland the last summer, I also found Waldo Bogle and his sister, Kate, now the wife of George Issit, formerly of Walla Walla. Waldo was the finest negro student I ever had. He owns a prosperous barber shop in the city, is married and has a son almost grown.

Ralph Brooks, with whose family I had dinner, is clerk at the Multnomah hotel, one of the fine hostleries of that city. It was a great pleasure to see and visit with many of these former pupils while there, as well as with Stella Croup Updegrove, Tassy McGillivary Sullivan, Mrs. Effie Yarnell, Babe Lynch Preston, the Holmes girls, Dora Chapper, Mrs. James Kidwell and some others whose names I do not now recall.

Alice Weir, now Mrs. Leo Stalls, is successfully teaching as principal of the Orchard Avenue school in this county. Carrie and the boys are all married and living elsewhere.

Of the Hunter family, I simply want to say that Fred, when he was grown, went to Los Angeles, where he engaged in the seed business. Later he moved to San Francisco, where he became quite wealthy. Just prior to his death a couple of years ago he said to his sister, Lillie, who was with him at the last:

"I should like to see Miss West. She was some teacher."

Lillie and her sister live in Spokane.

The Madlands moved to Seattle many years ago and have since resided there. Harry was in Alaska for many years, first as a merchant and later in the employ of the Seattle Hardware Company. Anna married and resides in Suquamish, in Skagit county.

There are many other families that I should like to mention. Some of them will be spoken of in the next article, while the others will remember that I think of them just the same.

It has been my policy not to mention many of the

girls who have married by name. I want to repeat what I have already said in a former sketch, that they are doing the greatest work given to a woman to accomplish, as home keepers and mothers.

CHAPTER XVIII

THE BAKER SCHOOL AS A MARRIAGE BUREAU

Forty-odd years ago, we had in connection with our seventh and eighth grade work a paper called the School News. This was edited each alternate week by a boy and girl whom I selected for the purpose. Every pupil in the school was expected to furnish some original item for the paper.

These were first turned over for my perusal as we desired nothin that would in any way hurt the feelings of a child. One day, much to my surprise, when the paper was read, the following ditty had found its way into the sheet without my knowledge:

"Whistle, Miss West, whistle, and you shall have a cow!"

"I never whistled in my life. How can I whistle now?"

"Whistle, Miss West, whistle, and you shall have a man!"

"I never whistled in my life, but I'll whistle if I can!"

155

It is needless to say that I never learned to whistle. Perhaps this accounts for my present lonely and forlorn condition. I have compensation in the fact that most of my pupils have taken warning from my fate and have married. Many chose for their helpmates those who also received instruction from me. These matrimonial ventures may have been brought about by their anxiety to escape such a fate. I am not so conceited, however, as to imagine that the fact of my pupils selecting each other was due to my training. Rather, it was due to that elusive little urchin, usually called Cupid, who is constantly shooting his darts to catch the unwary.

May I be pardoned if I give a roster of those who have done this so far? First I want to say that there is nothing more annoying to the teachers in these grades than the incipient love affairs which are constantly occurring.

In spite of the fact that a certain sympathetic mother informed me one time that it was wrong for teachers to interfere with the loves of boys and girls, I felt called upon to curb such tendencies wherever possible, because those so afflicted could not do their best work in the school room. I am frank to admit, however, that sometimes such affairs terminate happily.

Note the case of Adrian Broxson and Bertha West (no relative of mine). They were classmates and much drawn to each other even at that early date.

One day, I captured a note which Adrian was just ready to pass to Bertha. I opened it and read its contents. Then much to Adrian's relief I tore it to pieces and dropped it in the waste basket, remarking as I did so:

"Puppy love."

Many years later when I was visiting in Seattle, Adrian, driving a beautiful car, came to see me with his family, Bertha, his wife, and three fine children. He said:

"Miss West, I have come to show you the results of puppy love."

He is not without a sense of humor. Adrian is now engaged in the meat packing business in Snohomish but the family resides in Seattle where they have a nice home.

A. Franklin Kees, who was in one of my early classes, some years later found Susie Stetson just the girl designed to make their home a happy one. Frank is a good deal of a politician and has held many important positions in the state, the last being that of United States marshal for eastern Washington.

Glen B. Hite left Walla Walla a good many years ago and took up hotel work in Portland where he has been for a long time landlord of the Washington hotel. About 10 years ago, he decided he needed a helpmeet in his work. Returning to the home city he induced May Blalock to change her name and place of residence. They are now living at the Washington, which is the general stopping place for all Walla Walla people when they visit the City of Roses.

Phil Winans, cashier of the First National Bank of Walla Walla, coaxed Rose Blalock to be his wife. She died some years ago. Nezmith Ankeny of the same bank, not to be outdone, persuaded Edna Everz to help in guiding his life bark to the desired haven.

Dick McLean and Bonnie Jean Painter long since became one. Ike Laman induced Grace Jessee to go with him to Portland, where he entered business, doing well until he died some years ago. Grace has three fine boys.

Then there are Albert Bedell and Rowena Wydeck; Ed York and Sadie Harmon; Charlie Holloway and Grace Kenoyer; his brother, Harry, and Allie Fancher. Bob Sewart and Mamie Hamilton. All of them felt the call to surrender single blessedness for the joys of conjugal life.

Fay LeGrow, now a banker at Athena, Ore., decided that he had a preference for auburn hair. In consequence, he invited Jessie Bowles to share his destiny. John Brewer and his classmate, Jennie Markham, embarked together, while his brother, Frank Brewer, decided that as for him he much preferred Hattie Chew to any other girl of his acquaintance.

Hugh Phipps felt that Grace Allen was the only girl in the world. Both have long since passed to their reward. Ammi Crowell took Bertha Brewer for weal or for woe, while Will Hunter felt that Blanche Williams was the most charming girl on earth.

John Timmons captured Nida Coyle, but Byron Lutcher preferred Lizzie Coyle. Ed Shaw said that Maud Chadsey was the girl for him.

Charlie Chapman decided that he was fond of Frost and so induced Carro to travel with him through life, while Arthur Cornwell secured Carrie Ingram to preside over his home. Gerald Griffith asked the same favor of Jessie Colwell, and as dependable Albert Guichard wanted both sunshine and music in his home, he persuaded Lulu Gutheridge to furnish both for him.

Adrian Buys sought and secured Stella Picard for a wife. They have both passed into the great beyond. Julius Baldwin and Gertie Geisheimer married long ago. He is a printer of many years' experience and she just the housewife for him.

Rolla Proudfoot and his Fanny Gohlsen reside in Cowiche, where he is connected with a large creamery. Charlie McKean, still with his father in Walla Walla, married Bess Burford. His sister, Mattie, decided to keep house for Dr. Guy York, while Bess' brother, Harry, invited Eleanor Page to take passage in his ship of life.

Bob Ankeny persuaded Helen Brents that he was just the man for her, while Leland Crocker did the same with Beatrice Ryan. Fred Colt found Annie

Hawley a wonderful wife, and Ed Roberts is sure that for a better half Ada Coyle has no equal.

Milford Broughton had an eye for beauty as well as utility and so was insistent on securing Dana Bryant for a partner and guide through life. They live in Portland, Ore.

Grover Harris found Alta Kennedy all that could be desired as a wife. He recently died. George Gwinn and Rowena Evans made a match and lived happily until her passing years ago. Clifford Minnick induced Blanche Blackman to be his helpmeet and Tom Quinn is sure that Theresa Lyons is the finest girl on earth.

Will Coleman succeeded in Steel (ing) Margaret for his bride, Tim Paul secured Josephine Paine in the same capacity, while Jim Duff won Myrtle Gardner.

Will McLean could not find in the whole beautiful Walla Walla valley one who just appealed to him for a wife, so he "a-wooing went" and finally found in the Palouse country one who had not only gone to school to me, but lived in my home at Rosalia. Knowing my cheerless condition, she said "yes" when he propound to her the all-important question. Thus Allie Spurgeon escaped my fate and made him happy as well.

Have I named them all? Can you question the fact that the Baker school was indeed a veritable marriage bureau?

THE BAKER SCHOOL

I have been mindful of the fact that a long series of statistics is tiresome in the extreme and so have tried to make them as readable as possible. Even yet, the average reader will not care especially for them, but the old pupils may find interest in their perusal. I have been encouraged to give them because a certain cultured pioneer said to me just recently:

"Miss West, I didn't think I should care to read your reminiscences of Walla Walla, but I am finding them of intense interest."

His wife added:

"Yes, your stories are growing better and better all the time."

Of the 44 couples I have named, so far as I have been able to discover, the great majority have been happily married. This fact is noteworthy because one of the boys in writing me of himself recently said:

"You have asked me to tell you about myself. I am happy to say that even in these polygamous times in which we live I am the husband of but one wife."

There have been a lot of things I should like to say with reference to some of those whose names are here given and then, too, I have omitted a great army who went outside of the flock to secure their helpmeets for the life race. Many of these have done so well and are such worthwhile members of the great human family that I could literally fill volumes in relating their exploits and showing how they have been of real value to the communities in which they reside.

I am intensely proud of my boys and girls. Unlike the average natural mother, my "in-laws" trouble me not at all. They are all alike good to me and I am accorded a cordial welcome to their homes wherever I go.

Do not understand me to state that none of my old pupils have gone wrong. I could give you the names of some who have found the penitentiary a place of residence for a time. Others ought to have gone there. As a whole, they have become good, upright citizens and builders of creditable American homes.

May I remark here that the primary reason for the laxity in right living today, as I see it, is due largely to the fact that we are fast losing the American home. The automobile and the moving picture are rapidly taking the place of the evenings spent at the fireside with father and mother. Removal from parental restraint is a bad thing for the average boy or girl.

CHAPTER XIX

SOME TRUE STORIES OF THE WALLA WALLA PERIOD

Since the publication of the sketch on the Columbus day celebration I have received a letter from Alice (Cox) Lydon of Lewiston, Idaho, one of the worthwhile girls. She calls my attention to the fact that I had forgotten to mention that just the afternoon before the celebration, Professor Kerr decided that there should be a picture of Columbus himself on exhibition for the occasion.

Accordingly, Rachel Hamilton of the high school, who possessed rather remarkable ability as a pencil and crayon artist, was called to enlarge a small picture of the illustrious gentleman to place in the west front of the school building. Rachel worked diligently all evening and far into the night, in preparation of the sketch. She had it ready in time, but she was a little late getting into the line of march.

This picture was an exhibition for a long time in the school auditorium and elicited many favorable comments. I have already spoken of Rachel as now a professor of language in our state university.

I must not forget to mention the Smith family from Fort Walla Walla—Allen, Charlie, Margaret and Sue. They are the children of General Smith, now retired and residing in Spokane. Allen is a colonel in the U. S. army, Margaret is the wife of an army officer. The other two reside in this city.

Then there were the Paxton boys, Will, Harry and John, all fine fellows, and John Alheit and Ed Sauze and his sister Susie. Ed is now a patent office lawyer in Walla Walla.

The Besserer children, the Kirkman family, the Goodhues, the Knotts, the Brents, the Myslinskis, the McAlisters, the Jaycox, the Lasaters, the Parkers, the Brents, the Hungates, Ed Payne, the Lacys, the Bogles, Jas. Sykes, the Robinsons and many others too numerous to mention come to my mind. I never hear a name but I think that boy or girl went to school to me.

May I relate an amusing incident in this connection? Just a few months ago I noticed that one L. W. Rogers had delivered a lecture on theosophy in Norfolk hall in this city. I thought:

"That fellow went to school to me in Iowa."

As I was downtown, I went to the Davenport and

found him there, and it was as I imagined. That evening I went over to hear him talk. Soon after I went in a lady said to me:

"I am surprised to see you here."

When I remarked that the speaker had gone to school to me many years before, she asked:

"Is there anybody in the world who didn't go to school to you somewhere?"

There are literally hundreds of others whom I should like to mention, but I must forbear. Forgive me if I have left you out.

Everybody, old and young, likes a story. It has often happened when I was to speak to a company of people and asked what I should say, the answer has been: "Tell us a story."

My stories have the advantage of being true. I have determined to tell you some of them, which will illustrate, in part, my methods of securing discipline. You will remember that I have in a former paper spoken of the great lack of suitable discipline in our present day schools.

Dick McLean was a fine boy. I have never had one I cared more for, but he, like most boys, was inclined to be lazy. He didn't like to study. One day when I noticed he was wasting his time, I said to him:

"Dick, put on your hat and go ask your father why he sends you to school."

He went reluctantly, of course, and upon his return, I asked:

"What did he say?"

Dick replied: "To study."

Ten days later I was going downtown when I noticed Mr. McLean across the street. He motioned and I waited until he came across. Then he remarked:

"Miss West, I was mighty mad at you the other day."

When I asked the reason, he said:

"You sent Dick down to see me and ask a fool question when you know perfectly well what I would say."

I replied: "That is all true, but I wanted Dick to know, too."

He smiled and said that he believed I was right. After events proved that such was the case. I never again had to admonish Dick to study. He is now a prosperous business man of Walla Walla.

Again, I learned that the children were calling Professor Kerr "Pappy Kerr," while I was dubbed "Mammy West." One day I was in the basement and had occasion to step to the door leading to the playground. Just as I passed three little boys at the drinking fountain I heard one of them say:

"I wonder where Mammy West is going."

I turned and, putting my arm around him, asked:

SOME TRUE STORIES

"What did you say?"

"I said 'I wonder where Miss West is going.' "

Six times I asked him the question and each time he gave the same answer, growing more excited with each repetition until he was fairly shrieking his reply. Then I turned to the other boys and one of them said:

"He said 'I wonder where Mammy West is going.' "

Stooping, I gave the little rascal a hearty squeeze and said:

"For a long time Mammy West has wanted a little boy of her own and I am so glad to have one now, but I am sorry that Mammy West's little boy tells stories."

I took him upstairs, all the time with my arm around him, and, passing into each schoolroom, I introduced him to the teacher in charge as "Mammy West's little boy." This was effective, as I never again heard of any one calling me "Mammy West."

But, occasionally, I had to resort to the use of the "rubber shoe," famous in Walla Walla. When Mr. Kerr went to the high school he left a pair of his rubbers. For many years I used them as the instrument for condign punishment. Usually I gave the victim time to think it over. It often happened that the thinking was all that was needful.

Sometimes, in a case of really malicious wrongdoing, the culprit felt its efficacy at once. A case in point:

One day, during the noon hour, a small boy came to me looking like a ghost and telling me through his sobs how three other little chaps had misused him. Two of the boys had held their victim, while the third, holding back his shirt collar, had dropped a live mouse inside the shirt. It didn't take long to settle with the wrongdoers in a way they would not soon forget.

But another interesting case and its sequel:

One afternoon in the fall of 1884, just after I had called the school to order I noticed Will, a boy with auburn hair, in mischief. I called him out and gave him a seat in an armchair on the platform. Soon after, a dark-eyed little maiden in the rear of the room was also detected and she, too, was called out to stand near the desk until I had finished with the class recitation. Then I said to them both:

"Now, if you can attend to your work, you may take your seats."

Almost immediately thereafter I noticed a little wisp of red hair tied with a thread just under the chair where Will had been sitting. I picked it up and said:

"Will, does this belong to you?"

He gave an indignant negative, but Hallie, jumping

from her seat, and without permission, came hurrying forward and said in a partly audible whisper:

"Please give it to me. It belonged to my calf and I wanted to remember it."

You can easily imagine the merriment created and the anger of poor Will. During the entire afternoon we found it difficult to settle down to real work. Thus endeth the first chapter of the incident.

Some weeks later the Rev. D. J. Flenner, pastor of the M. E. church, came to the school building and said to me:

"Miss West, we are going to have a lyceum meeting at our church on New Year's eve and we want you to furnish something for us. At first I declined and then, remembering the story of the red-headed boy, I consented to prepare "A Schoolroom Incident."

After I had written it, I called Hallie to me at noon one day and read to her what I had written, asking if she cared if I used it in public some time. She said she would not.

Poor Will, who lived in the country, and who I hardly expected would be at the gathering, was not consulted. When the afternoon paper came out and Hallie saw I was down for "A Schoolroom Incident," she decided to spend the evening at home.

The church was filled to overflowing. When my name was called I went forward to the platform and, looking over the audience, noticed Will and his parents just in the center of the room. It was too late to retreat, and so I simply remarked that the incident had really occurred, but I did not say where.

As I read I noticed Will's face growing redder and redder until it rivaled his hair, while many of the pupils in the audience were turning in their seats to grin at him. When I closed in a round of applause, Mr. Flenner said, "Good."

Before I could take my seat, Ed Reed, the editor of the Evening Journal, stepped out in the aisle and took the manuscript from my hand as I passed. This was literally "the last straw," not only had I read it in public but it was to be published in the paper. His parents thought it a good joke but Will was raging and declared again and again:

"I will never forgive her. She made fun of my hair."

I was conscious of my mistake but nothing I could say to him had any effect in soothing his hurt feelings. He went to school to me until June of that year and while I never had any trouble with him, I could always feel that undercurrent of antagonism which I had unwittingly engendered.

He was something of an artist and I often found interesting little sketches of me lying around where I would be likely to find them. The last one represented Mr. Kerr and me sitting in armchairs beside each other. My head was upon his shoulder and he was looking down into my upturned eyes with a most languishing expression of countenance.

After he was grown up he went to Portland and entered the employ of the Oregonian where he was circulation manager for a long time. Perhaps 20 years later I was in that city enroute to San Francisco when I ran into him on Morrison street.

He came forward with beaming face and hands outstretched. We had a little talk and he invited me to have lunch with him. This I could not accept as I had a previous invitation. After lunch, I went around to the office and he took me through the plant, showed me the linotype machines and the method of electroplating, all of which was new to me and interesting.

He then took me to the ice cream parlor near where we had a dish of cream together. He had seemingly forgotten all about his anger over my really atrocious conduct and I was careful not to mention it. It is not many weeks since I had a friendly letter from him, written from his farm at Summerville, Ore.

When I published my little booklet for the old pupils 22 years ago, I was asked many a time why I hed left out the school room incident. The reason is obvious, but now that he has been pacified I am giving it here.

THE WIDE NORTHWEST

A Schoolroom Incident.

Pray indulge me, my friends, while I put into rhyme
Something very pathetic which once on a time
Created commotion, notwithstanding the rule
That no needless disturbance occur in the school.
The afternoon lessons are well under way.
Here and there a young urchin is slyly at play.
The teacher soon catches a boy with red hair
And at once says: "Young man, you may sit in this
    chair."
The culprit comes forth with a very red face,
And ruefully takes on the platform his place.
Very quiet he sits with never a look
For aught in the room save only his book.
All is still for a time when the teacher espies
Slyly at mischief a young miss with dark eyes.
"That girl may come here," and at the command,
Near the desk, she blushingly takes her stand.
Thus for near half an hour with order restored,
The lessons proceed, while the teacher deplored
The need that compelled for discipline's sake
Of offenses like this she notice must take.
The punishment over, to their seats they've returned,
When on the floor near the chair, the teacher dis-
    cerned
A small bunch of hair, neatly tied with a thread.
In color a most unmistakable red.
Very natural conclusion: "The boy owns this hair,"
And so again is called to the chair.
When the curl is presented, vehement his "No"

SOME TRUE STORIES

And angry his actions as to his seat he doth go.
The dark-eyed little maiden, then leaving her seat,
Comes at once to the teacher, looking modest and
    sweet,
Very shyly she whispers: "Please give me the hair,"
While blushes seem burning her features so fair.
The smile of the teacher and an audible laugh
Quick forced explanation: "It belonged to my calf;
The poor little creature is but recently dead,
And I want to remember it," the little maid said.
Her treasure recovered, the maiden seems glad,
But the boy with red hair appears very mad.
The school sees the joke and at once raises a laugh
To think the boy's hair looked like that of a calf.
The noise has subsided. And now I would fain
Draw the curtain in silence, although it is plain
The boy's feelings are injured. It was mean to com-
    pare
The covering of a calf with his beautiful hair.
This story a moral, I am sure, must possess,
But the best way to find it I'm frank to confess
Has puzzled me much so I leave it just here
And wish one and all a happy New Year.

    January 1, 1885.

CHAPTER XX

SEVERING MY CONNECTION WITH
THE BAKER SCHOOL

In the summer of 1900, when the teachers were elected for the following year, I gave notice that this would be my last year in the schools. I had purchased a farm at Rosalia. I planned to go there to live and "go back to the farm," as people say today. Then, too, politics and religion had crept into the school board. I never believed in such a mixture in our public school work. Either alone would have been bad, but the mixture made what seemed to me to be an impossible situation.

The work began as auspiciously as usual and was carried on through the year without much friction. Every little while I heard it hinted that the board was after Superintendent Kerr's scalp and confidently expected to get it. He, however, felt that while it was not material for him to remain longer, he wanted to be reelected and then resign. I could not make him see how foolish he was in the attitude he had assumed. He said:

"I am sure of three members of the board and then, after I am elected, I shall just present my resignation."

We talked over the situation many times, for he was a frequent visitor at my home. I could not influence him in the least.

I had no difficulty in disposing of my home, and with that off my hands I was free to begin the erection of a home in Rosalia, where I expected to live. My farm was but one mile from the town.

I had on the whole a competent corps of teachers and felt that we were doing good work. It is interesting to note that Mrs. Josephine Corliss Preston was my primary teacher and was generally recognized as most competent in her work. She is now state superintendent of public instruction.

It was, I think, in this year that one day at the noon hour a boy came to me in the primary room, where nearly all the teachers had assembled, crying and telling me that Walter Fancher had hurt him. I sent for Walter.

Soon he stood before me, looking as all small boys look when they have been guilty of wrongdoing. Now, the boy's father was a South Methodist presiding elder and a fine man. I looked severely at the culprit and asked:

"Walter, what is going to become of you?" '

He replied:

"I am goin to be a preacher."

And when I told him that the Methodist people would not have him for a preacher unless he learned to do right, he naively remarked:

"I ain't going to be a Methodist preacher."

"What are you going to be?"

"A Baptist preacher."

Can you blame me for letting him off that time? He certainly showed a considerable amount of wisdom for so young a boy.

I had secured rooms with Mrs. George J. Buys, with whom I had boarded for seven years, and here I lived for a period of seven month. It was during this spring that I celebrated my 50th birthday.

I mention this because that day Mrs. Jack Jones, who had been one of my teachers for a considerable period of time, invited Mrs. A. S. Bowles and me to dinner. During my absence the folks opened my rooms and when "Tab" (I always called Mrs. Jones that) rather hastened my departure from her home, much to my indignation, I found upon my arrival at my rooms the place brilliantly lighted and the whole house overflowing with guests.

On the dining room table glittered fifty dollars' worth of beautiful cut glass, the gift of the church young people and the Sunday school with which I had been connected during my 18 years of residence in Walla Walla. It was a delightful surprise and showed a degree of appreciation which was wholly unexpected.

May I say here for the benefit of those who so often are tempted to tire in well-doing, because of the seeming lack of appreciation, that often, if you presevere, you secure that appreciation when you least expect it. There is much truth in the saying:

"Cast your bread upon the waters, and after many days, it will return to you.

I have proven it true again and again.

About May 1st Mr. Kerr came to see me one evening and said:

"Well, the board will meet tomorrow night and I have three members lined up who are certain to vote for me."

But I still was not convinced and urged him to put in his resignation. He refused to do so, saying they had each promised to cast a vote in his favor.

He felt that it would be in a sense an acknowledgment of his efficiency in his work. He would then resign and all would be well. The eventful evening arrived.

One of the members of the board was called to the country to see a patient, while a second was unexpectedly called out of town. Unfortunately, they were both Mr. Kerr's friends. When the vote was taken, it stood two to one in favor of electing another man as superintendent of the city schools.

As I have already stated, the political boss had sent me word through Mrs. Margaret Center, the efficient school clerk, some days prior to this, that I could have my position if I wanted it. I had declined and my name was not considered. Had it been, I should likely have lost my head the same as Mr. Kerr.

I feel that it is due to Mrs. Center to say in this connection that she was for many years our school clerk and was always honest, competent and conscientious in her work. Years after I left there, I am told the ax fell on her defenseless head.

Perhaps an hour after the board adjourned, I saw Mr. Kerr coming to tell me the news. He looked to be 75 instead of his real age of 52. It was a terrible blow to his pride and he never recovered from it.

The student body held indignation meetings and passed resolutions expressing confidence in him. All to no avail. He left Walla Walla with the avowed purpose of never entering its portals again.

Thus passed out of the school life of Walla Walla one of the most scholarly men I have ever known, his single lack being the inability to discipline others. He had become a decrepit old man while yet in his prime. He retired to his home farm in Pennsylvania and in the few letters I had from him he always expressed bitterness at the injustice which he could not overcome.

SEVERING MY CONNECTION

When a year ago last summer I wrote and had several of the old pupils write as well, urging him to come out to Seattle and I would gladly share the honor of the annual reunion with him, he replied that he was physically too infirm to make the trip. It was not long thereafter that we heard of his passing on the same farm where he was born 75 years before.

Just prior to the close of the school year a company of my friends gathered at the home of the Rev. H. B. Turner and tendered me a reception. A committee of the teachers was present and before the evening closed they gave me a little testimonial which I prize highly.

It is in the form of a small booklet in red leather, upon the back of which a picture of the Baker school has been burned, while inside there is the picture of the high school and the following lines:

"Walla Walla, June 14, 1901: The teachers of the Walla Walla public schools, kindly remembering the efficient and self-sacrificing services of Miss L. L. West in the cause of city schools and many personal favors, present this as an expression of their esteem and friendship. To learn of her continued success and pleasure will be a great delight."

It was signed by G. S. Bond for the Sharpstein school; Mary J. Thomas, Baker school; Rachel E. Hamilton, Paine school, and J. W. Shepherd, high school.

Thus closed my work in the Walla Walla schools extending over a period of more than 18 years. In many ways they were the happiest and most successful years, from a monetary point of view, of my life. I formed many friendships which will be a comfort to me through my life.

It is a joy to feel that I can go back there at any time and find many people who are ready to give me a cordial welcome, whose homes are open to me. May I relate an amusing incident right here?

Several years after I left Walla Walla I was invited by Mr. Bond to return and speak at their county institute, an invitation I was glad to accept. I was downtown when I met Mr. Goodhue, the express agent, whose office was in the N. P. railroad depot.

As we walked up street conversing, I, of course, met many people who knew me and I stopped to speak and shake hands with each of them. When we reached his office, he said:

"Never again will I walk up the street with you."

In surprise, I asked the reason, and he replied:

"I have had to take off my hat to every man, woman and child we have met on the way and I have taken cold in my bald head."

The morning I was to leave Walla Walla I had a message from my brother, stating that the Rosalia school board had been to him to ask if I would take charge of their school the coming fall. I replied in the affirmative, upon certain conditions. These they agreed to and so my farming scheme "went a glimmering," never to be considered again seriously.

Before taking up the Rosalia chapter in my life work, however, I want to write a sketch of Whitman college, as it seems this period of my life would not be quite complete without speaking of this great school and my relations with it over a long period of years. As you already know, I was associated with its founder, the Rev. Cushing Eells, at Colfax and later with Dr. Anderson and finally with its present president, Dr. S. B. L. Penrose.

CHAPTER XXI

WHITMAN COLLEGE AND ITS
RELATION TO THE PUBLIC SCHOOLS

I has seemed to me that the record of my work in Walla Walla would be incomplete without some mention of Whitman College for the reason that I was in an early day so closely associated with its founder, the Rev. Cushing Eells, and later, to a greater or less degree, with the three presidents of the institution, since it became a college. In the beginning, may I quote from the writings of another?

"Twelve years after the Whitman massacre, there came one day to stand at the grave of Marcus Whitman at Waillatpu, another missionary who remembered what Dr. Whitman had done to save the country to the United States. This man, small of stature, mild of manner and speech was Whitman's closest friend, Cushing Eells, a man of most romantic history.

"Born in Massachusetts, a graduate of Williams College in 1834, for 55 years a missionary, he was called the St. Paul of the Pacific Northwest. Standing by Whitman's grave, Eells resolved to build the fittest monument to a man like this—a school for boys and girls who some day will be here.

"He sold half the farm he had taken up and gave the money for a school building. He peddled cordwood, chickens and eggs, while his wife made butter for the school. For a time he lived on dried salmon and water at an expense of 25 cents a week to save money for the school. He gave Whitman seminary, as it was first called, $10,000 and made it his residuary legatee. A great minister in the east said of him in the year 1883: 'He was the most Christly man I have ever met. I regard him as one of the saints of modern times.'"

After the school became a college in 1882, Dr. A. J. Anderson, then president of the territorial university at Seattle, resigned and became its first president. Dr. Anderson was a man of fine personality and an executive as well as a teacher of rare ability. He made the school a power in the community and surrounding country but a period of financial depression occurred.

About this time the president resigned. He was succeeded by the Rev. James F. Eaton, who served the school for three years. Dr. Eaton was a man of fine presence but he was an eastern man and seemingly could not adapt himself to the spirit of the west. Finances were at low ebb and it seemed that the school must die. Dr. Eaton resigned.

Fortunately the Rev. Stephen B. L. Penrose was near at hand as pastor of the Congregational church at Dayton. He was called to the presidency. This was in 1894.

I well remember talking with a friend of the school, perhaps a month prior to his call, and as we discussed the prospects of the school, pro and con, I remember saying:

"There is just one man who, if available, can, I believe, save the institution from death and that man is the Rev. Mr. Penrose."

I was greatly pleased when I heard not long afterwards that others had felt just as I did and that he had been called and had accepted the task. It was a stupendous undertaking to lay upon his shoulders. We all know how well he succeeded in building up and making it a great school.

Then when he came to take up the work and moved with his bride into the house adjoining my own home I was greatly pleased. We lived in adjoining houses for three years and I found them fine neighbors as well as delightful friends.

I have always looked upon him as one of the really great educators it has been my privilege to know. Not only this, but he is a man af rare ability as a pulpit orator. He is one man whose presence inspires confidence. His wife is one of the most charming women of my acquaintance. I count myself fortunate, indeed, to number them among my personal friends.

WHITMAN COLLEGE

When Dr. Penrose took over the presidency of the institution in October, 1894, it had 34 students, only two of whom were in the college. The remainder were in the preparatory department. The faculty consisted of five members. There were three old wooden buildings, a campus of six and one-half acres and a debt of $12,500.

There were some bright spots in the cloud, however. The school had an excellent reputation. Just at this juncture came an offer from Dr. D. K. Pearsons of an endowment of $50,000 on condition that the school raise an additional $150,000.

No steps had been taken to meet this magnificent offer from a great man who had been profoundly interested in the romantic story of Dr. Whitman and the attempt to found a college as a monument to his memory.

I am one of those who believe that when the All Father has a great task to accomplish he raises a man or a woman to accomplish that undertaking. He never makes a mistake. He had been fitting Dr. Penrose for just this task in his preparation for the ministry and his work with the Dayton Congregational church.

Just as George Washington undertook the task of leading the continental forces to victory, so Dr. Penrose took over the job assigned him and led on to victory in raising the desired amount to secure the first permanent endowment for the school. It was a task seemingly almost as difficult of success as the leading of the ill-fed, poorly paid army to securing the independence of the American colonies.

The Lord of Hosts led in each case and the work was done. He had a job to do. He tackled it alone. Then, calling to his assistance the right-minded people of the great Inland Empire and elsewhere, he was able to put over the "seemingly impossible."

Right here I want to correct an error in the published prospectus of the college, date 1924. The error is found in the statement: "When Whitman College was chartered, Seattle and Walla Walla each had a population of about 7,000."

As a matter of fact, when I went to Walla Walla in 1883, one year after the granting of the charter, there were, including myself, just 11 teachers in the public school. We did not average 50 pupils each. Multiplying the possible 600 pupils by five, a too-liberal estimate, we could not have had a population of to exceed 3,000, less than half the population given in the quotation.

All the more honor, then, to the school which has grown from 34 students in 1894 to more than 600 the last year.

This article would not be complete without mentioning some of the really remarkable assistants who have helped Dr. Penrose in his great enterprise.

The first I want to mention is Professor W. D. Lyman, who taught in Whitman for 54 years. He was a scholar, a writer and a fine instructor. It was my privilege to take a series of lessons on the works of Shakespeare under his instruction. Professor Kerr used to say:

"Lyman is the most remarkable man I ever knew. He can sit in our men's literary club apparently fast asleep as some one reads a dry, prosy paper. Then, when he is suddenly called, he rises to his feet and begins to talk just where the other fellow left off."

Then there are Professor L. F. Anderson, who served as an instructor for a period of 42 years; Professor Helen A. Pepoon, 31 years the dean of women, and Professor H. S. Brode, with a service of 24 years. It is proper to remark here that Professor Brode enjoys the distinction of being the father of triplets, three boys now grown to manhood and successfully "doing their bit in the world." I hope the good "daddy" will forgive me if I tell an amusing incident concerning these three boys.

They were lively little chaps. One night when the parents went out to attend some sort of a function a young girl was left in charge of the children, who had been put to bed. The girl was instructed not to disturb them unless she heard some noise in the bedroom.

A little later she heard a great commotion in the bathroom and hastened to see what was the matter. The enterprising young men had stripped the bed of clothing, crowded it into the bathtub, turned on the water full force and then they too, got into the tub. You can well imagine the result and how difficult the poor girl found the situation.

There are others of the professors who might be mentioned, but I am speaking only of those whom I have known personally and well.

Dr. Penrose, during the many years of my life in Walla Walla, was ever ready to assist in our teachers' gatherings. In this way, he exerted a powerful influence upon the work of the public schools.

He has now been at the head of the college for more than three decades. No one can measure the value of his great work there nor that of his exceptionally fine wife. May I conclude this article with the words of Professor W. A. Bratton relative to Dr. Penrose?

"To speak of the faculty, students and alumni of the college as "the Whitman family" has been a favorite expression of President and Mrs. Penrose and to all of us who have enjoyed the fragrance of their friendship these are no empty words. We experienced their beautiful hospitality, which has not meant just an occasional dinner or reception, but a cheerful room and bed and kindly care in sickness, a quick recognition of loneliness or discouragement and a happy way to cure it, a best friend's interest in our marriages and our babies, a real pleasure in our successes, and time both to counsel and to help.

"There is no home of any one who has been connected with Whitman in the last 20 years in which the home life is not finer because of the sane wholesome family of the Penroses. I know of no man with whom I can so thoroughly and so pleasurably disagree on so many points as with Dr. Penrose, but they are points only, without dimension.

"The great continuous current of his purpose and life has my profoundest admiration, and I am sure I express the sentiment of our whole faculty when I say that we count it among our greatest blessings to have had part with him in his great work for this college and this section."

CHAPTER XXII

ROSALIA

I little thought when I first saw Rosalia in 1879 that it was ever to be my home. Yet such it was for a period of more than six years. It seemed to me on that hot, dusty, July day that it was the most dreary, desolate place I had yet seen in the Inland Empire.

The town at that time consisted of the J. M. Whitman store, his hotel and the big barn which still stands. Some years later my brother purchased the Whitman homestead. His widow now resides in the house Mr. Whitman built for his third and last wife. He was a marrying man you will observe.

The house, remodeled, makes a comfortable home. Much of the farm has been sold until now only a few acres remain. Rosalia was for a long time the stage station where the driver changed horses en route from Colfax, the metropolis, to Spokane Falls, as "the friendly city" was first called.

I shall pass over my arrival at my new home, my getting settled in the "house of seven gables," as I had named the home built for my occupancy prior to

190

my coming, and my trip to California. That was one
of the conditions exacted before I would begin the
work of the school year. It is proper to say at this
point that a major reason for my leaving my delightful work in Walla Walla was the fact that because of
a sensitive throat I felt it important to get away from
the fogs of the Walla Walla valley for a time at least.

The school equipment at Rosalia was none too good.
The building was old and dilapidated. We had no
laboratory. I found it a novel experience to change
back from the grades to high school work again. The
changes in natural science had been surprisingly great
in the nearly 20 years I had been teaching in the
grades. I found myself a good deal of an ignoramus
along the lines of physics, especially as much of the
knowledge of electricity and its application to so many
industries had been developed during that period.

It was quite a come-down from 600 children on my
hands every day to 150. It was a welcome relief just
the same. In the main, I was given an excellent corps
of teachers. Miss Louise Luenberger, Now Mrs. J. L.
MacDonald of Spokane; a Miss Naomi Williams, later
Mrs. Frank Anderson, and Miss Cora Goodnight of
Spokane were all well qualified for their work.

My first assistant was a flat failure and caused me
considerable trouble. I shall not mention his name.
He was sore because he was in a subordinate position,
ignoring the fact that he was only a second-grade
teacher. After some months we let him go. With the
assistance of some of the high school girls we man-
aged to get through the year with credit.

I learned this, however, that it is much easier to work in a large school than a small one. I had a class of six high school girls who were a real joy to me. I shall speak of them again in closing this sketch.

In these girls I was able to verify my belief that one can do much more for a child if you have him, or her, under your supervision for a considerable period of time. For this reason I am not in sympathy with the present departmental system of teaching. You lose much more in the line of discipline of the child than you can possibly gain in extra efficiency of instruction coming from experts along any certain lines of work.

It was during the summer of 1902 that I allowed myself to be inveigled into running for the office of county school superintendent. I strenuously objected at first as I had only been back in the county a year. Besides M. C. McCroskey, the incumbent, was a candidate for reelection. The McCroskeys were and are legion in the county.

When I was nominated by the big convention at Colfax without effort on my part, I felt that I ought to accept. This I did to the tune of $250, for I was defeated by a majority of 300 votes.

My defeat was brought about by a certain political boss. He went back on his promise to me and supported Mr. McCroskey by turning to him the votes promised to me in order to secure one of his pet candidates for another office.

ROSALIA

Later, I was not sorry for the defeat as it left me open to accept a position paying $25 a month more than the superintendent's salary. I confess to feeling just a little sore at first. This put a quietus on any further political aspirations on my part, although I have thought sometimes I should rather like a whack at the legislature. There are some things in our state school laws which I should like to see changed. If I were on the inside I might help to accomplish the change.

The second year opened auspiciously with Miss Clara Pengra of Oregon as my first assistant. She proved much more satisfactory than the man had been. Miss Luenberger left us at Christmas. This left a gap in our ranks hard to fill for she was in many ways a remarkably fine teacher. We found a substitute in Miss Helen Wyland, and the work went along smoothly until the end of the year.

So far as I know, only one couple enrolled as my pupils in Rosalia decided that they were well adapted to go through life together. The young people are Ellis Stone and Edith Kennedy, both coming from pioneer families.

John Kennedy, Edith's father, came to the country among the first white settlers to arrive. He still makes his home in Rosalia. The Stones have been for many years counted among the great wheat farmers of Whitman county.

Fred Stone, the older son, a good many years ago married Theresa Worthington, one of my finest girls.

She, like her mother, believes with Roosevelt that it is a womans duty to rear a large family of children. If I am not mistaken in the count they have nine to their credit and are really an ideal family.

May, another of the Worthington girls, is now a widow and resides in the town. She is looked upon as the standby in all kinds of good work.

F. J. Wilmer, the banker and state senator, has resided in Rosalia for years. His four delightful daughters were enrolled in my school, as were their cousins, the Trainors, several of whom have become successful teachers. I had rather planned at one time to have Mary Trainor for a niece but the young folks decided otherwise and so I could not insist.

Then there was Dr. Leonard, the pioneer druggist, one of nature's noblemen. It was my privilege to teach his boys. I always think of him in connection with the early growth of Spokane for he said to me many years ago:

"Because of the porous soil, Spokane will always be an unhealthy place. They can never have a really good water supply."

We little thought then that the city was to grow to such an extent that it would be necessary to bring the water supply from wells east of the city.

The Donohues, the Andersons, the Campbells, the Brockways, the Turnleys, the Riggs, the Mulkays,

ROSALIA

Jesse Williams, the Choates, the Bournes, the Wests and many others were the backbone and sinew of this thriving community which has come to be the best town in Whitman county, outside of Colfax and Pullman.

But going back to the school. At the close of the year I graduated from the tenth grade with suitable exercises five of the six girls to whom I have already alluded. Bessie Settlemier dropped out before the end of the year. Evaline Boozer, Martha J. Merritt, Reta M. Roberts, Lena L. West and Lily Wyer passed creditable examinations and were given diplomas for the work accomplished.

It is interesting to note that we had two evenings devoted to the graduating exercises. At the first, the girls each gave an original essay and we had a public reception on the second evening at my home which was well attended. I wrote and had published as a greeting from the girls to their parents and friends the following lines:

> Commencement time, auspicious day—
> A milestone reached on life's highway.
> We pause to greet our friends so kind;
> Ere we seek out the nooks designed
> For us to fill. It may be fate
> Shall bring us influence large and great,
> Or that stern abiter may decree
> Our lots in life must humble be.

THE WIDE NORTHWEST

A larger school we now begin—
A school where, 'mid the busy din
Of ceaseless bustle, constant care,
We're called to seek for jewels rare.
We may not know. Tomorrow's sun
May tell of victories grandly won,
Of conscious growth, of added power;
Or adverse clouds may darkly lower.

*　*　*

The fairy hope, with magic hand,
Beckons to heights where we may stand
Among the stars, and, standing, know
Life's difficulties lie below.
Ere these be reached, we each must climb
By rocky path, and many a time
Our hearts will waver and grow chill,
And yet we must press upward still.

*　*　*

Thus moving steadily year by year,
With hope to guide and faith to cheer,
Eyes fixed on love, the perfect grace,
We're sure at last to win the race.
And when the highest goal is won
And all our lessons have been done,
Life's fruitage gathered, and at hand,
We'll seek with joy Immanuel's land.

ROSALIA

Dear friends, we come to you tonight
With grateful hearts and prospects bright.
We thank you for the loving way
In which you've led us, day by day.
The years to come alone can tell
If we our work in life do well.
We know you've done for us your best,
And now 'tis ours to do the rest.

★　★　★

These girls are all, so far as I know, happily married and in homes of their own are living out woman's
highest destiny, that of wife and mother. It has remained for my niece, Lena, to make up for the de-
linquencies of her old aunt in this direction, for she
has in her home three stalwart boys and an equal
number of charming little girls. She still resides in
Rosalia, but the others have made their homes elsewhere. There are many others of the Rosalia pupils
whom I should like to mention.

It is proper to add that Ross Alverson is now the
surveyor for Snohomish county of this state. He has
a charming wife and two children.

CHAPTER XXIII

REPUBLIC AN OLD MINING TOWN

When I closed my work in Rosalia in May, 1903, and took account of stock, I discovered that I had actually been in the schoolroom for a period of 48 years. I began school at 4 years of age, and during all this period I had never had any respite from shcool, except the long summer vacations.

I had taught during several of them. Surely, I felt, I was entitled to a year off. So I rented my home and made arrangements to spend a winter in California with relatives and friends.

It is interesting to note that prior to my leaving for the golden state I decided to spend a little time in Walla Walla, visiting friends there. I mention this because of the fact that during the three weeks I spent in that hospitable city I spent 21 nights in 21 different beds and had my dinner , in 21 different homes. My readers are admonished to beware how they "go and do likewise."

I was really worn out and my digestion had been

somewhat impaired. One Sunday when I dined at the home of F. S. Dement and remarked at the dinner table that I had been obliged to turn down four invitations to dinner that day, little Frank said:

"I should have gone and eaten them all."

By the way, Mr. Dement was for years a member of our city school board. I found him a kind friend as well as an efficient officer always.

I shall pass over the winter spent in California until March. One day I received a letter from Republic. It proved to be from the school clerk. He stated that they had been having a good deal of difficulty with the discipline of their school and that I had been suggested as a suitable teacher to straighten out the tangle for them.

Would I accept the principalship of their school the coming year? I had really planned not to teach any more, but the opportunity appealed to me. A little later I wrote that I was returning to Washington in April and would make a trip to Republic and look over the field before giving them a definite answer.

This I did. Before leaving the town I had signed a contract to return in September and take charge of their school at a good salary. I was thus able to do what I had wanted to do for a long time—print and send to my pupils a booklet, of which I have spoken in a former sketch.

THE WIDE NORTHWEST

The environment of Republic is a veritable beauty spot. I never tired during the two years of my life there of feasting on the magnificent scenery and in enjoying the delightful climate. Although it was cold in winter, it was the still, dry cold that is not at all hard to endure.

There was much snow, but all winter long it lay upon the stumps of trees, there not being sufficient wind to blow it off. The wonderful fir and tamarack trees laden for days with a thick covering of snow were beautiful beyond description. It was Bryant who said:

> "To him, who in the love of nature
> Holds communion with her visible forms,
> She speaks a various language."

The school building was in a valley, some distance below the level of the main street. It was my custom when I climbed the hill, to turn and drink my fill of the beauties that surrounded me. This was notably true that first fall after my arrival to take up the work.

The foliage was beautiful, furnishing all the colors of the rainbow. In the winter the yellow tamarack, among the green of the pines and firs, presented a surpassingly charming picture.

I found about 250 pupils in the school, most of whom were possessed of the rather lawless spirit characteristic of most early day mining towns. Do not understand me to say that there were not a good many fine children and many fine people in the com-

200

munity. I am speaking of the conditions as I found them in the school. The children had apparently been allowed to run wild. It was my task to bring order out of chaos.

The teachers, six in number including myself, were ready to assist as best they could but it remained for me to bring the children to realize the importance of obedience to authority. A case in point:

I found the walls of the hall much spattered and stained with the snow balls of the preceding winter. I was particular with the coming of the first snow to forbid the snowballing of children as they entered the building.

The first morning after a snowfall, I looked from my office window and discovered three boys doing what I had told them not to do. The young gentlemen were marshaled into my presence. Each in turn suffered condign punishment. This had a most salutary effect upon the school as it happened that one of the offenders was the son of a member of the school board.

They learned thus early that I was no respecter of persons. Another case in point:

Soon after the opening of the morning session of the school, Miss Dale, my first assistant, sent for me in haste. When I opened the door, the stench was something awful. Miss Dale remarked:

"Some one brought limburger cheese to school this morning and it has been thrown into the register."

Ordering the windows opened, I talked to the nearly 50 children in the room, keeping my eyes fixed upon the class for evidence of guilt. As I talked of the enormity of the offense which brought discomfort to so many people, I noticed, as I expected, certain boys who appeared uncomfortable. I said:

"You and you and you may come with me."

Now it is a fact that most children are unable to conceal guilt from one who has become an expert in reading faces. The boys all assured me of their innocence but it wasn't long until I had trapped one of them into giving himself away. He in turn soon incriminated the others.

Then they told me how one of the boys had brought the cheese to school and got the others to help him deposit it in the registers and in this way cover up the guilt of each other. I shall draw the mantle of silence on what followed. It is needles to say we had no more of that kind of thing.

Just one other case, although they might be multiplied many times that first year:

I discovered that the children had a habit of snowballing everybody who passed without regard to age or sex.

One afternoon, as I dismissed the school and stood in my office window watching the children as they passed out, I noticed that they broke rank at the end of the walk and began a wholesale snowballing of

REPUBLIC

Mr. Galley, an old gentleman who made his living picking up old rubbers and the like for sale.

I saw one boy throw a ball which hit the old man. They saw me and dispersed in a hurry. The next morning I went to each department and told what I had seen the night before and said:

"Now, I am not going to tell you the boys I saw hit Mr. Galley, but it will be well for you to confess by standing up. Otherwise, it will be unpleasant in the extreme for the guilty one who does not admit his fault." I rounded up 10 boys and that morning I began the day by administering 10 samples of corporal punishment.

The high school was small, never exceeding a dozen, all told, but they were a really fine class of young people. Some of them I have lost track of but there are several who have become fine, up-to-date citizens. I find Herbert Kippen, a successful business man in Seattle, and his sister in business in Portland, Ore. Ralph Hunner is also in business in Portland.

Stanley Fairweather is in the mining business in Mullan, Idaho. Fred Radigan and John Finn are here in Spokane. Fred Lowrey is in California. Tom Finn is in Stevens county.

Enith Hunner married and still lives in Republic. The Thompsons have married and gone. Eva Hane is superintendent of schools for Ferry county and charming little Miss Robinson was still in the Ferry county schools at last accounts. There are others I should like to mention but I forbear.

Of the social conditions of the town I need only say they were the aftermath of what was once a live mining community with all the sins and general lawlessness of such a place fully rampant. It takes time for a community to settle down to normal after such orgies of general wrongdoing.

Republic was no exception to the rule. Many fine people, yes, but we had four saloons! This was just four too many in a town of our size. When I tell you that a physician of the town said, "It takes just what I make in my practice to pay my poker bills," you can imagine something of the conditions. That man had a family, a fine one, but his wife made the living for them.

As I neither danced, gambled nor drank whisky, my sources of amusement were not many outside of my work. However, we had a woman's club which met at regular intervals. I arranged several school functions which were well received.

I walked much, for, as I have already stated, I was entranced with the magnificent scenery of the place. We had church, too, a supposedly Baptist institution, I am ashamed to admit, for although the pastor was an able sermonizer, I had little use for him in other ways.

At his earnest solicitation I took hold of the Sunday school with the understanding that I was to be permitted to run it on regular lines. He constantly interfered. Finally, when at Christmas time, I remained to put over a program for the children, instead of going to have the holiday dinner with my brother's family, the pastor brought in at the last moment a woman of dissolute character and demanded that she be permitted to sing. He carried his point but I quit then and there.

As I have already stated, there were many fine people in the town. I recall with much pleasure the John Stacks, the Thompsons, the Robinsons, the Tompkins, the Fairweathers, The Stockings, the Walshes, the Becks, the McFarlands, the Harpers, the Hurleys, the Grant Stewarts, the Ritters and some others, including a number of bachelors, all of whom were good friends of mine.

During the second year I had as my first assistant Miss Marie Stack, who deserves more than passing mention. So far as I know, she is still teaching and is in many ways a remarkable woman.

But much to my pleasure, I found that the owners of the Tom Thumb mine, several miles out from town, had sent as caretaker for the mine Dement Church, who, because of ill health, had been ordered to the mountains. His wife, Bertha Ballou, was an old-time pupil and a mighty fine girl, as are all my girls.

It was my privilege to spend the day a number of times in their cabin home at the mine. Then, too, over at Curlew, a few miles away, near the lake of that name, lived the Hunner family. The son and daughter

Ralph and Enith, were in my high school class. I spent a number of week-ends with them and with the elder daughter, Mrs. Guy Helphrey, than whom there is no finer woman here below. The Hunners and Helphreys now live in Sandpoint, Idaho.

I found W. T. Beck, president of the so-called "Hot Air" railroad, a real friend.

It was the dream of his life, as well as that of some other people, to build that road down the San Poil River into Spokane. Like many other air castles, it was only a dream.

Nor would I forget the Heglands, with whom I boarded the last year of my stay in Republic. Mrs. Hegland was a wonderful cook and prided herself upon the fine dinners she served, especially on Sundays.

I recall when Watson C. Squires and Wesley L. Jones visited us (Mr. Jones had just been elected United States Senator). Mrs. Hegland was most anxious to surprise the distinguished guests with a wonderful dinner. Even I was drafted to make the salad for the occasion. Strange, isn't it, that an old teacher knows how to do such things? It is true, nevertheless.

CHAPTER XXIV

WAR TIME WORK IN ELTOPIA

When I closed my work in Republic I was fully
persuaded that my teaching career was at an end.
This was not to be. I shall pass over a period of
years when I was not actively employed in the school
room. All the time I was busy in educational work in
one form or another.

I taught English at Spokane university for several
months, gave health talks, visited and talked to
schools and was a member of the teachers' examin-
ing board. I felt that I was never really out of har-
ness as I had planned to be.

In the summer of 1917 a friend, living on a dry or
desert farm in Franklin county, wrote me that the
school board at Eltopia wanted to secure a mature
and competent teacher for their schools. She had suggested me. Would I come and look over the place
and decide if I were willing to accept the appoint-

ment? In accordance with this request, I went to Eltopia, met the board and, before leaving, signed the contract to return in September and take charge of their school.

It is interesting to note the origin of the name of the town. Just prior to the building of the Northern Pacific railroad through the place, a well had been drilled which furnished an abundant supply of excellent water. This made it a stopping place for freighters between Pasco and Spokane.

One night two men arrived. After they had the evening meal they began to gamble. Ere long one of the men had won all the money the other had and wanted to quit. The loser said:

"Nothing doing. I am going to win some of that money back before I sleep or there will be hell to pay."

This phrase was given the English pronunciation and the town became "El-to-pay." The railroad, when the time cards were printed, called it Eltopia. So it has been known ever since.

The country for the most part is a desert waste, but with water it will rejoice and "blossom as the rose." When the Columbia river basin project is a reality this place will become a veritable paradise because it has the climate, soil and everything else to make it a wonderfully productive section.

I found a fine school building, virtually new, costing some $16,000. It was reasonably well equipped and

WORK IN ELTOPIA

well adapted for our work. The old building had been fitted into rather crude apartments for the use of the teachers.

I was given two assistants, a Mrs. Davis of Walla Walla and Helen Blankenhorn of Spokane. We had about 50 pupils, some eight of whom were in the high school. Three young men and a young woman were in the 12th grade, supposedly. It was only supposedly, however, for I found them deficient in English but well up in other subjects. They were Lawrence Stredwick, Maurice and Joe Hollinsworth and Lucy Baxter.

Before the close of the second week I said to the class:

"Now, if you want to graduate from the 12th grade in May, next, you must do intensive work in English."

This they said they were willing to do. I told them I would require a theme each week on some designated subject, besides other work in teaching them to speak and write correctly. I shall not soon forget the sorry work they made of it the first week nor how, on the second attempt, the boys all fell by the wayside.

I said to them:

"Boys, I am here to direct your work. I know what you need, but I am no hard negro overseer. I shall gladly help you in every way possible, but you must come to time or you can not graduate in May, as you desire."

This put a new light on the situation and they went to work. Fortunately, about this time Mrs. Emmer, who was my landlady for more than a year, was so unfortunate as to lose by death a fine-blooded rooster which had been given her by Captain McCaffrey, the head of the road section crew. This was a serious loss to her, but a real godsend to me, for I seized upon the demise of the fowl as a help in my English class.

On Monday morning I said to the class, after giving a largely imaginary sketch of the life of the departed Major McCaffrey, as I called him:

"Now, you may write for your theme on Friday next a eulogy to be delivered at his funeral."

This tickled the fancy of the boys and they went to work. A week later I said:

"I am pleased with your effort. Now I want a suitable obituary to be inscribed upon his tombstone."

"The third week we had a biographical sketch of his life and the fourth week a sermon to be delivered over his mortal remains. I was much gratified with the success of this scheme. I had no further trouble in teaching the class English.

Joe, who had seemed to have the most difficulty in the first place, became so enthused with the work that he wanted to be at it all the time, to the exclusion for his other studies. I was able to graduate the whole class the following May, but insisted upon each of them writing and delivering an oration in public at the close of the school.

WORK IN ELTOPIA

I wrote to the state college and secured the admission of the three boys into the freshman class without examination, with the understanding that if they made good no examinations would be required. Lawrence Stredwick worked his way through the school and graduated with honor.

Maurice also graduated and is now married and living in Portland, Ore. Joe left school to take up surveying and is doing well. Lucy attended a summer school and secured a good second-grade certificate to teach. She is now married and is in all ways a fine wife and mother.

I am telling this story because it may be a help to some sorely tried teacher in interesting her boys in the study of English. Appeal to their imagination in some such way as this and you will be surprised with the results obtained. A really successful teacher must be something of a genius in the matter of invention.

I was invited to remain a second year but the other teachers dropped out. I was given two new assistants who in the main proved satisfactory. This was the year of the "flu" epidemic and the school was more or less disrupted thereby. Some weeks prior to the close of the school year I was obliged, because of illness, to give up the work and return to my home in Spokane.

There were some unpleasant features about the work in Eltopia. I found two distinct factions opposed to each other. If you were friendly with the

211

one, you were "at outs" with the other. This made it hard but there were a few fine people who proved to be true blue.

In them I found solace from the loneliness which otherwise would have been intolerable. I mention Mr. and Mrs. Emmer, with whom I boarded the last year. They are really fine, outstanding people. Mr. Emmer owns the well to which I have already alluded and supplies the village with water. His place is virtually the only real green spot in town.

The Druens next door to them are fine people. Mr. Druin has the only store in Eltopia.

Harry Brown, the postmaster, has been on his job for many years. He is a character in his way and is said to be one of the most careful and painstaking officials in the service of the government. One of the inspectors for the postoffice said to me that his reports were always just as they should be.

The Thompsons, the Russells, the Phends, the Libbys, the Stredwicks and a few others now make up the town's population. There has been a considerable falling away in this respect since I left there. Mrs. Ina Butler, a daughter of the Thompsons, one of my assistants my last year there, is now county school superintendent and has been elected for a second term.

Mr. Vauter, the station agent, has been at his post for a long time. Although he has a crippled hand, he is considered most efficient and is well liked by the company.

This sketch would be incomplete without mention of C. D. Miller, who was president of our school board for some time. He is quite domestic in his tastes and loves his home dearly. Because of unfortunate circumstances but through no fault of his, there had been a separation between himself and his wife. I am telling this because I proved to be a successful matchmaker.

Today he is happy in having one of my own girls for his wife. I am assured that he and Blanche are happy in their home life and both are able in a measure to forget the sorrows of the past for Blanche lost her first husband by death and a little later her only son. The marriage is a source of great satisfaction to me for I had come to have a high regard for Mr. Miller.

This is one of the richest school districts in the county, in fact in the state. They are able still to employ three teachers at good salaries, although most of the children are transported from the country and now only number about 30, all told. This is illustrative of the inconsistencies of our school law.

Because of a large number of miles of railroad track, this school has plenty of school money, while neighboring districts, with more children, are hard pressed for funds. This defect can only be remedied, as I see it, by turning all taxes from railroads into the general

213

school fund and then apportioning them to the districts on a per capita child basis rather than as it is done at present.

I am not knocking Eltopia when I say this, but the system, which impresses me as most unfair. We find the same condition to exist in Marshall and elsewhere in the state.

My readers never can fully appreciate this section of Washington until they are permitted to experience one of the rather frequent dust and sand storms which occur during the summer months. They are awful. That is the only way to express it. They always reminded me of the placards which were posted all over the country at the time of the building of the Northern Pacific railroad. They read:

"Keep you eye on Pasco."

The first time I visited Pasco, I said:

"The wording is all wrong. It should read: 'Keep Pasco in your eye.'"

Then, too, the heat of the long summer days is something to be reckoned with, but as I have already said, the winters are delightful in every way.

In my next sketch I shall take you across the mountains and spend a couple of years with you on Camano Island, in Puget Sound. Of this place the wife of a distinguished Presbyterian clergyman said:

"It is the only place I have ever been in my life where I was obliged to reside in a $700 house and have a $10,000 view."

CHAPTER XXV

CAMANO, THE BEAUTIFUL

When in the spring of 1919 I was obliged to surrender my work in Eltopia because of what the doctors said was high blood pressure, I returned to my home in Spokane. In August, however, I was able to go to Olympia for my teachers' examination work. That fall I went out for the superintendent of public instruction, securing statistics for the department and giving talks to high schools as a side issue.

In a period of seven months I visited 27 counties in the state and spoke to 25,000 high school boys and girls. It was a delightful privilege, especially as in every instance I was invited to come again. There were many interesting incidents connected with this venture which I should like to narrate, but I must not tire your patience.

In the fall of 1922 I moved downtown into a small apartment and began to do private tutoring. When I

215

learned that the legislature had passed the teachers' retirement act and that I must be teaching if I desired to avail myself of its provisions, I wrote to the superintendent of schools in Island county, asking him about a small rural school where I could go back after 50 years, to rural school teaching. I felt that it would be better for me to spend a year on the Sound if I could secure a position there.

This letter led to my accepting the Camano school. This town is located on a small island of the same name and is some 12 miles from Stanwood in Snohomish county. When the tide was in we were on an island, but when it went out we were on the mainland. A steel bridge connects the island with the mainland and so we were nicely situated.

The island is 18 miles in length and from one-half a mile to three miles in width, extending north and south. Camano is on the west coast, about midway of the island, and has a population of some 75 people. It is on Saratoga channel, the inner passage of the bay, which separates the island from Whidby. That is the principal island of the group and is some 60 miles in length.

Few large vessels ever attempt this inner passage, as the turbulent water of Deception pass are hard to navigate. The channel is about three miles in width. The wooded hills on Whidby present a surpassingly beautiful picture. I never tired of it when the weather permitted them to be visible. I shall close this sketch with an apostrophe I wrote the first winter. It will give you some conception of the beautiful scenery of this section of our wonderful country.

We had daily connection with Seattle, some 60 miles away, a small steamer arriving each evening. In December our dock went out in a gale and thereafter we were reduced to the train and bus service from Stanwood for communication with the outside world.

The people are poor and, as in all small sections, they do not pull together. So the building of a new dock has held fire ever since. Seventy years ago the island was densely wooded.

Now it has been mostly logged off. The land is not of much value, except for gardens and chicken raising. However, much small fruit of various kinds is raised.

The first year I rented a small cottage and lived next door to the hotel. There was in my yard an abundance of apples, pears and plums. One large apple tree furnished most delicious Gravensteins for the whole neighborhood as long as they lasted.

A. E. Frizzell conducted the postoffice and a store here for a long time. He has now retired and has gone into the chicken business, having an up-to-date institution right in the village. They were among my warm friends and Mrs. Frizzell showed me many kindnesses. Mr. Rensaler now has the store and also a number of boats for rent.

August Blomquist, with whose family I boarded during my last year in Camano, lives just one-half mile from the village. They were wonderfully kind to me. Indeed, I doubt if I could have gone through the last year had it not been for the kindly ministrations of Mrs. Blomquist. She is one of nature's noble women. When I was so unfortunate as to contract the "flu" that spring, she mothered me in fine shape. I shall never forget her.

The school board members, Harry Oleson, J. C. Russell and John Johnson, were kindness itself. Mr. Johnson and his good wife were specially kind, taking me in their car to Coupeville, our county seat, and to Stanwood a number of times. Their three children did good work in the school. Six-year-old Robert began his school life with me. By Christmas time he was reading and writing well and from that date he never missed a word in spelling for more than a year and a half.

Mr. Russell proved to be a most efficient clerk. We had a good building, fairly well equipped. I enrolled about 25 pupils each year of my stay in the school.

I have long believed that English is the most important work in the teacher. In consequence, I majored in that subject in my work. I had one fine little fellow, Gus Ross by name, but he couldn't spell and he did not know how to construct sentences.

One day I sent his class to the board and dictated this sentence for them to write correctly:

"Henry Wadsworth Longfellow is sometimes called the household poet."

Gus wrote:

"henry w. long felo is somtim caled the hoshold pullet."

The poet didn't rise in his grave to protest, but we had a good laugh at the expense of poor Gus. Let me say for the young man that he made commendable progress. He moved into another district the following winter and so I did not have opportunity to give as much help as I should have liked.

I had one little fellow who had gone to school the whole of the year and had learned nothing. His mother came to me and said:

"Now, Harry doesn't seem to be able to learn, but I have to send him to school anyway."

It wasn't many days until I discovered that his fault was inattention and a lack of perseverance. Early in November I found he was able to read a little and I gave him some writing exercises. Then one day I said to him and to Robert, to whom I have already alluded:

"Now, boys, I am so old-fashioned that I want you to learn the letters of the alphabet, capital, small, and the script as well."

They went to work with a chart before them each day. When the test time arrived Robert gave a perfect lesson, but Harry fell down in part. I gave Robert 10 cents for the performance and Harry 5 cents.

After Christmas I began putting simple words, six in number, on the board each morning and before the boys left for home in the afternoon they were required to spell the words correctly. Robert never missed, but Harry was unable to spell more than two or three correctly. Finally I said to him:

"Harry, I want you to go out and get me a switch."

This I placed on my desk and then told him that I had no desire to use it, but I felt I should have to hit him once for each word he missed. It had the desired effect. For weeks he never missed a word and his eyes always shone with pleasure as he was dismissed.

Later I knew his mother was going to Seattle to visit the father, who worked in that city, I suggested that she take Harry with her for the week-end trip as a reward of merit. This she consented to do.

On Monday after his return he missed a word. He had had his vacation and had nothing to look forward to. Again I resorted to the stick, and this cured the young man so that during the second year he rarely missed a word. He was promoted to the third grade.

I am giving this story for the benefit of some sorely tried teacher who is at her wits end in the endeavor to persuade some negligent pupil to secure results. My experience is that most pupils can learn if you can induce them first to give attention and then to apply themselves to the task in hand.

Before the end of the year my salary had been raised and I had been invited to remain another year. This I consented to do, although at the outset I only planned for one year of teaching. I had become interested in these, for the most part Scandinavian children, and wanted to help them to learn to use the English language, if possible.

Fortunately, in the spring of the last year, Mr. Hall of the First National Bank of Stanwood sent out letters inviting the children to write a theme of not to exceed 250 words on the purpose and need of a bank in a community.

I put the little folks to work and not long before I left I sent to Mr. Hall some six or eight themes written by my pupils. A few days after I reached Seattle, en route home, I had a letter from Jennie Karo, a sixth grade pupil, whom I had promoted to the seventh grade, in which she said:

"Dear teacher: I just can not wait to tell you that I have just had a letter from the bank and they have sent me a check for $10, the first prize, and Beatrice Adams won half the second prize."

Later I learned that Reta Rowe, another of my girls, had won the other half. Thus my pupils had successfully competed with a large number of schools in the community and made a clean sweep of the prizes offered. This was ample compensation for the patient and persistent work of teaching these young people to use language correctly.

As in every place, I found some fine people here. I must mention just a few of them and tell a little something of the kindly fashion in which they treated the teacher. Miss Eccles, who had the hotel next door to my first home, was a most competent and hard-working woman. The hotel had little or no patronage. She turned her hand to anything she could get to do. Then Mrs. Lizzie Baker, across the street, was a real joy in many ways.

One day, not long after my arrival, I had just returned home from school when there came a call and I went to the door. Mr. Gardner said:

"Where do you want your potatoes?"

He had brought me a 100-pound sack of as fine spuds as ever were raised. Another day Mr. Russell brought me a fine large head of cabbage and said:

"If you want blackberries, go to my garden and help yourself."

Again, one evening, H. V. Thompson brought a bag of all kinds of vegetables. Mrs. Thompson was our school clerk the last part of my sojourn in Camano. I found them the finest people, ever ready to lend a helping hand wherever possible. Indeed, Mrs. Thompson served in the late war as a trained nurse. She is really the doctor for the entire community.

Again, Mrs. Frizzell appeared one evening with nine glasses of delicious jelly. I must desist or you will come to think I never had either to buy or cook anything in the eating line. Suffice it to say that they were extra good to me.

CAMANO, THE BEAUTIFUL

I may not name them all. I will simply say that while the scenery and the climatic conditions were all that could be desired, that the old gentleman with a cloven foot of whom we read sometimes had somehow found his way into the community. There were some "black sheep" in the Camano flock. The mantle of silence shall cover them and their deeds, so far as the writer is concerned.

The crying need of our rural schools is to give the children something worthwhile with which to occupy their leisure time. I bought checkers, dominoes, flinch cards, authors, anagrams, puzzle maps and various mechanical devices for the school. It was an interesting spectacle to observe the children at a long table in the rear of the room engaged with one or the other of these games.

We had a book social, asking each one to bring a book for a circulating library. The Seattle library gave us some of its old books and Mrs. E. D. Laman, a good friend of mine in Seattle, gave freely to the children.

The last Christmas of my stay she sent me a great package which contained a gift for all and even the babies of the town. Ray Passage, a business man of Seattle and one of my boys, sent two boxes of beautiful oranges, marked: "For you and the kiddies."

We were able to report a circulating library of some 200 volumes when I left the place.

In closing, I want to give you the opostrophe to which I have already alluded:

THE WIDE NORTHWEST

Camano

All hail to thee, Camano, Isle of the Inland Sea!
Dame nature, ever prodigal, has show'red choice gifts
    on thee.
Thy hills, thy fertile valleys, thy shrubbery and thy
    trees
Sing peans of praises when swayed by the salt air
    breeze.

★   ★   ★

The silver sheen of thy mornings, the warmth of thy
    noonday's sun
And the golden glow of thy evenings, when the daily
    tasks are done,
Bring peace and a quiet pleasure, presaging that sweet
    rest
Which comes to the weary pilgrim as light goes out in
    the west.

★   ★   ★

All hail to thee, Camano, and to thy wondrous bay—
A jewel set in emerald! Its shifting scenes each day
Fill the soul with rapture and the heart is led to
    praise
The good and kindly father who leads in all life's
    ways.

CHAPTER XXVI

AFTER FIFTY-FOUR YEARS—DID IT PAY?

After 54 years, did it pay?

Had I been asked that question a quarter of a century ago, I should have answered: "Yes, with reservations." Now I am able to give the affirmative answer, "Yes," without reservations.

I have had a great light these last few years and there has come to me a vision of the nobility and usefulness of the real teacher. You will note the statement, for there is today a great army of so-called teachers who are simply school keepers. To them can come none of the true joy experienced by one who works with the impressionable and plastic child mind, not of necessity the individual child, but of the whole human family and especially the junior part of this family.

Some one asked me just recently: "Why is it that

your pupils remember you so kindly and seem glad to do so many beautiful things for you? So many others fail to receive anything like the same consideration. I do not remember a single one of my own teachers that I feel the same way toward."

I replied: "The answer can be given in a single word of four letters. My boys and girls knew instinctively that I cared for them and so the single word, love, tells the whole story."

Just as a natural parent has sometimes to punish his or her child, so the universal parent must do the same, not from the love of punishment, but because of the scripture injunction which says: "Whom the Lord loveth, he chasteneth." The real teacher stands in exactly this relation to the disobedient child.

Could you have watched Harry Joy when I visited him in Portland last August you would have realized something of the truth of this statement. He was a naughty boy quite often, and I punished him many times, but with shining eyes he said to me: "Oh, Miss West, I am so glad to see you. I know I was a bad boy, and I am sorry for it now," not a feeling of resentment was in evidence during my entire visit with him, but only regret that he had wasted his time, and was not able to hold the positions which had come to his younger brother and sister. He has, however, developed into a fine man and is doing his bit in the world with a reasonable degree of success.

In contrast with this, a so-called teacher, not many miles away from this place, after attending a certain enjoyable function to which she had to take a number of her pupils said: "Really, a teacher has some nice times, if she didn't always have to be troubled with a lot of little brats." This unfortunately is not an exceptional case. Literally thousands of teachers in our grade and high schools, our normals and our colleges, are imbued with the same false notions—men and women who pose as leaders of youth, who are profane, intemperate in their habits of speech, and in many ways show their contempt for the young people they are expected to lead into planes of higher living.

We have for many years been letting down the bars along moral and spiritual lines, and then we wonder and are aghast at the laxity in uprightness of character so apparent in our young people of today. Believe me, the teacher as well as the parent is largely responsible for this deplorable condition, and I can not but sound the warning of the good book, which so many so-called higher critics claim to despise, "As a man soweth, so shall he also reap."

Just this last summer I heard of a certain professor and this on credible authority, who is accustomed to calling his students fools, blockheads and many other objectionable epithets. He is actually profane in his remarks, and this because some of the students are not able to measure up to his demands in their recitation periods. He is so conceited as to assert that there have been no real English scholars since the time of Shakespeare, except himself, of course.

THE WIDE NORTHWEST

If I had my way, that man would ere many days be invited to seek other avenues of human endeavor, and yet an all-wise board of regents allows him to practice his arts upon a defenseless student body, which must recite to him. This is no imaginary case, but an actual fact.

But, going back to my subject, I want to give you a few of the reasons why it has paid me to be a teacher of youth all these years. Let me quote from a letter received not so long ago: "I shall pause in the great stir of life to tell you some of the things that are in my heart for you. I was 9 years old when I entered Baker school. As the years rolled around I became your pupil, and I never had a more worthy teacher. Through the 41 years that have passed since then, I have loved you for your sterling worth."

Last August a colored man and his sister came to the hotel in Portland to see me. The next day there came a letter enclosing a $5 bill. The general, said, for I always called him general because of certain outstanding traits he possessed, "The visit we had with you has made us happy. With best wishes for your continued success, and hoping to ever remain in your memory, we are lovingly yours."

And yet another just received: "I am happy to think that we, your old pupils, will have the privilege of possessing a book from your pen. I do pray for the success of your great undertaking. It must succeed. May the babe of Bethlehem be near you this Christmas time." I could quote from many others, but these are sufficient.

A large number of men and women all over the country who have made a real success in life have assured me that they owed their first start on the way to me and to my influence upon their lives.

Should you go to Colfax, you will find upon the site of the little building where I taught that first school, a fine $25,000 church. Enter its portals and you will observe a beautiful memorial window, put there by my old pupils and friends of that early period.

Could you have attended the wonderful banquet tendered me a little more than five years ago at the Hotel Davenport, at which more than 100 of the old pupils and their families were present, have seen the choice flowers, partaken of the delicious menu, listened to the delightful speeches and the letters from the absent ones, and then heard the speech when I was given nearly $400 with which I might purchase a diamond ring if I so elected, been assured by a letter from Charlie Dement of the kissing episode that he had rather kiss me a thousand times now than Howard Knott once, you would have been led to exclaim as did the colored woman in charge of the wraps: "Your old scholars shore think a heap of you."

Then could you have gone with me as I visited 27 counties of our state and spoke to great throngs of high school children, and have witnessed the enthusiastic reception accorded me everywhere, and could you have heard the cordial request to come again from every place, and could you have heard many say, as did Charles Henry at Pullman, "I must congratulate you on your ability to talk to the hardest class of people in the world, and hold their undivided attention," you would then come to believe that it has paid me royal dividends to have taught all these long years and to still be able to command this attention even in this "jazz" age, to the things which are really worth while.

Ere I close, I am going to let you into a secret of my life. For a number of years it was my ambition to be a physician. I read medicine for more than a year and many times I was urged to give up my work and enter a medical college, but the lure of my work was ever present and I stayed by it, even when it was most discouraging. Today I am inexpressibly glad that I did so.

I should probably have made more money in the other work, but I could never have come in touch with so many human lives, and I can say today that all the wealth of John D. Rockefeller or a Henry Ford could not purchase from me the feeling of joy and satisfaction which fills my heart as I contemplate the goodness of the great arbiter of human destiny who kept me steadily at the task which he had assigned me to accomplish.

AFTER FIFTY-FOUR YEARS

One of our great poets said:

"Men may come and men may go,
But I go on forever."

May I paraphrase it and say:

Teachers may come and teachers may go,
But I am the pioneer forever.

It is proper that I give just a bit of advice to the young at this point. You are living in the most marvelous age in the world's history. Avenues of human endeavor are opening up to you such as were never before vouchsafed to mortal man. It is for you to go forth and accomplish the seemingly impossible.

"There are thousands to tell you it can not be done;
There are thousands to prophesy failure;
There are thousands to point out to you, one by one,
The danger which will surely assail you.
But just buckle in with a bit of a grin,
Just take off your coat and go to it;
Just start to sing as you tackle the thing
That can not be done, and you'll do it."

I close this series of sketches with a feeling akin to sadness. It has been a real joy to open up the storehouse of memory and live over again the incidents of the past. Many people have assured me that they enjoyed what I have written, but I want to assure them that mine has been the greater joy, for "all of this I have seen, much of this I have been."

[THE END]

APPENDIX

MISCELLANY

Explanatory—During my long life as a teacher in Washington I wrote a large number of addresses, and some poems, part of which I am impelled to publish in this volume because they in a sense give some idea of conditions as they existed in the past of our great state.

MISCELLANY

MORAL CULTURE

At the first institute held in Colfax in May, 1880, I read the following address which was later asked for publication in the Journal of Education, bearing date October, 1884.

The term, as I here use it, does not include the development of the religious faculties, for although I regard training in this direction as of vital importance, I recognize the fact that it will not do under existing circumstances to introduce religious teaching into our public schools.

Every right thinking person, however, must admit that it is highly important that children receive careful conscientious training in those things which pertain to strict integrity of purpose and uprightness of character. The teacher, from my standpoint, has an important mission in this respect, for surely in this day and age of the world such training is more needed than ever before. Young America is a proverbially fast youth. A boy who spends his time as a street corner loafer with a cigar between his lips and a good stock of oaths with which to embellish his conversation is every inch a man in his own estimation. When he has added to his other valuable acquirements the ability to drink and gamble, he is a finished gentleman. Nothing more is needed to complete his education.

Such is the goal to which many of our boys aspire. They do not all reach it, but alas, so many are carried to such a depth in the vortex of sin and folly that they are but wrecks of what they should have been, and many others are hopelessly overwhelmed.

Our girls, too, are in danger; though the goal to which they would attain is different, it is still an objectionable one. A young miss who can use slang fluently, can simper and gush about her beaux, and who spends what time she has to spare from these absorbing duties in considering the question of dress, or whether bangs or crimps are most becoming to her style of beauty, feels that she is a charming and accomplished young lady. Unfortunately it does not end here, for she is looked upon as a model to be imitated by her associates.

But it is not with these faults and vices that we, as teachers, have so much to do, and which we are so particularly called upon to combat. There is a growing tendency to dishonesty, untruthfulness and deception in small things, and it is of these that I wish now to speak. Many persons say because a fault is of a trivial nature it is unnecessary and unwise to notice it. But it takes little grains of sand heaped one upon another to form the mountain; moments make up the year and just so the little acts and thoughts and purposes piled one upon another must make up each individual character for weal or woe.

A teacher may in a certain sense be likened to a potter. A child is placed in his hands. The mind is soft and easily moulded. Neither good nor bad habits have taken deep root. The careful and judicious teacher may uproot the bad, and may plant those seeds which shall germinate and bring forth a goodly harvest of pure thoughts, noble acts and temperate habits. And he, the teacher, may turn out from under his instruction a beautifully modeled and rounded life, at least, one having no unsightly blemishes.

There is the more need of teachers exerting an influence in correcting the bad habits and erroneous ideas of children because in so many homes, they, who should be guides in morality and truthfulness, are just the reverse. How many times I have heard a mother promise her child that which she had no intention of granting, but to quiet its persistent asking, she assented thinking it would be an easy matter to revoke her promise when the time came, or that the child would forget all about it. How many times I have heard parents unblushingly and unhesitatingly tell their children what are called white lies and that too, when the lies were so transparent that the children could readily detect them. Only a few weeks ago I visited a lady who is the mother of five beautiful children. One day in conversation she remarked proudly. "I am a model mother." A short time afterwards I heard her make this remark. "It is necessary to lie to children. I often promise my children things that I never mean they shall have." It seemed to me her remarks hardly harmonized. Under such influences children must early imbide habits of deception, and must form a low estimate of the value of truth. But it is not my province to write a treatise on the deficiencies of parents. I have to do with teachers, and we as a class have not, I fear, reached a point where we can say, "We are holier than you."

I have intimated that our duties as teachers call us to correct more particularly the habit of deception, untruthfulness and dishonesty in small things. Let me now enumerate briefly some of the ways in which teachers foster the very habits that they should seek to uproot. One of the chief ways in many of our schools is the self-reporting system. At the close of the day each pupil's name is called and he is expected to report conduct for the past six hours. "Perfect" is the almost universal answer. But if the teacher has had eyes and ears during the day, he knows that perhaps only one in a dozen who have given this answer is really so, and yet many of the others don't mean to lie about it. The fault was so trifling, such a little thing, surely it was excusable, and could hardly be considered a fault. Thus the conscience is quieted, but little things grow rapidly larger, and a habit of deception is fixed that does much to mar the future life of its possessor. Much better that the wrong doing remain unreported than that the child be taught to try to cover it up and thus double his transgression. Another way in which teachers injure their pupils is by making threats or promises and then failing to carry them out. This is often done. Teachers are often addicted to the same bad habits they seek to uproot in their pupils. A teacher who swears, smokes, drinks or gambles, cannot hope to make his boys see the impropriety in these things. "Like begets like," and very probably the pupils will soon be almost as proficient as the teacher himself in these manly accomplishments.

Could we realize but a tenth part of the responsibility resting upon us as guides and preceptors of the young, how much more careful we would be; how much harder we would try to make our lives worthy of imitation. Permit me to close this article with the hope that we as teachers may be more thoughtful about these things, that we may study how to help our pupils to build noble characters for themselves. By so doing we may be led to polish and beautify our own lives until in this respect we may approach perfection.

More than forty years ago, I was invited to address a public meeting in Walla Walla on the "Teaching of Temperance in the Public Schools." The address follows but first let me say that after I had concluded the address and a number of people came and commended me for the effort, one small boy who stood by, pulled my dress and when I stooped to find what he wanted, he whispered: "I got pretty tired of it truly."

THE WIDE NORTHWEST

TEMPERANCE TEACHING IN THE PUBLIC SCHOOLS

1887

(Prepared by request of the Walla Walla W. C. T. U. and read at a public meeting.)

Three thousand years ago, because of the sins of the people, the wise man was constrained to write: "Wine is a mocker, strong drink is raging, and whosoever is deceived thereby is not wise." And again, he writes: "Who hath woe, who hath sorrow? Who hath contentions, who hath babbling? Who hath wounds without cause? Who hath redness of eyes? They that tarry long at the wine; they that go to seek mixed wine. Look not thou upon the wine when it is red. When it giveth his color in the cup, when it moveth itself aright. At the last it biteth like a serpent and stingeth like an adder."

Did he live in these, our days, think you he would make a milder protest? Ah, no! All his wonderful power of expression; all the force and brilliant imagery of rhetoric would be called into operation to thunder and re-thunder forth the words of warning. In all ages of the world there have been worshipers at the shrine of king alcohol. No county, no locality, I might almost say no family, has ever been free, at least in a civilized country, from the evil contaminating effects of this demon; coming in pleasing garb to rob its victims, physically, intellectually and morally, and to bring the poor deluded ones to drunkard's

graves. But it has been left to this glorious nineteenth century, this period of time during which so
much has been accomplished in the way of science,
of literature, of art, and of human advancement generally, to witness the crowning act of man's degreda-
tion and debasement as well. Never was there a time
when the rum power had such a hold as now. Never
a time when he could marshal his hosts by the millions
and ten of millions as he can today. Never a time
when so many were filling drunkard's graves as this,
the end of the most marvelous century the world has
ever seen. Think of it friends, 60,000 men and women
die every year in these United States from the effect
of strong drink; 5000 every month, 166 every day, and
while we sit in the room this afternoon seven souls
are carried into eternity with the words of divine
wrath ringing in their ears: "No drunkard shall inherit
the kingdom of God." But the evil ends not here,
think of the heart broken wives, the mourning mothers,
the destitute and often homeless children left to fight
the battle of life without their natural head and pro-
tector. Think of the destitute homes the insane asy-
lums and penitentiaries filled to overflowing with their
helpless victims. Think of the corruption and fraud in
private and in public life chargeable at its doors, and
then we can begin to measure the awful evil of this
thing we call strong drink. It robs our homes of that
which makes home bright and beautiful, the father's
loving protection, the mother's tender, watchful care.
It robs our schools of the means needful to carry on
the work of education, and worse than this it implants

within the boys and the girls certain inherited tastes and desires for that which defiled the parent that can never be uprooted and destroyed.

It robs our churches of many who might otherwise become useful, honored instruments of God in the salvation of souls and the means whereby the church may obey the divine commission: "Go ye into all the world and preach the gospel to every creature." It robs society of its pure moral tone, the physcial and intellectual culture that should embellish and adorn all the social relations of life.

It robs the nation of its brightest and best. Unfortunately it is not alone the unlettered and lower classes that are tainted with this plague. It is found in high places as well—in the governor's chair, on the bench, in the councils of the nation—its victims are counted by the thousands, and are held in a bondage worse than death. The political corruption of the world is appalling. Read the recent newspaper articles concerning the governor's mansion in New York and you have a picture of the drink and tobacco power in high places in our own country.

Go where you will, north, south, east or west, you cannot find a locality, scarcely a home, where the baneful effects of alcohol are not seen. The cry of the widow and the orphan made desolate by strong drink is everywhere heard.

Our jails and our penitentiaries are more than full of its victims. In the Illinois state prison some years ago 1300 persons were questioned as to the causes that brought them there. Over 900 responded, "strong drink." It is fair to presume that in our own fair city and commonwealth the proportion is as great or even greater than this. Should you enter the jail beneath us and go to the prison on yonder hill you may count the victims of king alcohol by the scores. But you need not go to this trouble. As you leave this room and walk the main street of our beautiful city simply notice the men you meet, the blear eyes, the inflamed nose, the unsteady gait, and untidy clothing; all tell the same old sad story. All speak of one cause, a cause producing everywhere the same terrible effect.

One thousand millions of dollars are spent every year by king alcohol in his work of distruction and death. One hundred and forty millions for public school purposes, thirteen millions to carry the gospel to the heathen. Think of it my friends, for every dollar we spend in fitting the young for the responsible duties of life more than five dollars are spent in dragging souls to perdition; for every dollar we send in spreading the gospel among the heathen $77.00 are used by the emissaries of alcohol.

What a record for a Christian country, a country so blessed and favored of God!

How justly might the doom of the drunkards of Ephranni be pronounced upon us:

"The crown of pride, the drunkards of these United States of America shall be trodden under foot. And the glorious beauty, which on the head of the fat valley shall be a fading flower, and as hasty fruit before the summer which when he that looketh upon it seeth, while it is yet "in his hand he eateth it up."

It is claimed that for every heathen saved by the missionaries in Africa, one hundred of his fellows are destroyed by strong drink. We furnish the missionaries; we furnish the alcohol. How long will it take Christian America to evangelize the world? Can you solve the problem?

But it is my province to deal with the teaching of temperance in our schools, public and private, and to answer the question, should such instruction be given and how? First let me say, that I believe most earnestly in temperance in all things that in any way relate to the healthy preservation of these marvelous bodies of ours, these temples of the living God, and because of the dreadful curse entailed upon the human family by tobacco and rum, I cannot but believe in total abstinence so far as they are concerned.

Why then should children be taught temperance and total abstinence principles in our schools? Because many of them receive such instruction no where else.

Of the more than twenty-one million children in the United States, fewer than half are in the Sunday School. Many of our boys and girls are surrounded by home and family influences that foster rather than check their evil propensities. It is only in the day school that these come in contact with the noble and refining influences and principles needful to build them into a complete symmetrical manhood, or womanhood. Every young person is largely moulded by his environment. The taint of a degraded home life, or of evil associations cling to him through life. The public school, and the public school teacher must assume this herculanean task of attempting to counteract these influences. It becomes the duty and privilege of the teacher to take these lumps of unsightly clay, so full of defects and to tenderly, patiently, and lovingly mould and fashion them into vessels meet for the Master's service. Why should they do this? Because in the young is centered the hope of the future. The church, the state, the nation must in the next generation be manned by the boys and girls of today, that they must occupy positions of responsibility and power none can gainsay. If they are to well and faithfully discharge the duties which will devolve upon them, they must be educated, and that education must be complete and symmetrical in every detail. It must have to do with the threefold nature, the physical, the mental and the moral or spiritual. Each of these must receive due attention else our young people will grow up one-sided, narrow-minded men and women.

The physical well-being of the child is pre-eminently important. Suitable exercise must be encouraged; mental development is of little use when the body is weak and frail. Abstinence from all things hurtful to the system must be urged both by precept and by example. Young America is a fast youth. The young Washingtonian may be classed among the fastest of the fast. The force of circumstances makes him so. Do not suppose from this statement that I consider our young people and children worse than the average. Far from it. No truer-hearted, broader-minded, kindlier boys and girls have I ever known than those I have called my pupils in this town, but we live in a fast age—in a specially fast section of country. The stirring, exciting bustling life in this far west creates a thirst for stimulants. The boy sees his father indulging in his after-dinner pipe, or his glass of liquor. That father is his ideal of manhood. The boy would be a man, he must do as father does or he shall never reach that high estate. This is one of the things the public school teacher must seek to counteract and to show by precept and example that the principle is an erroneous one. In doing this she must be as "wise as a serpent and harmless as a dove," else the vials of parental wrath are poured upon her defenseless head. Did you ever think, friends—you whose habits are more or less intemperate—that the pernicious examples you thus set before your children are laying the foundation stones for their disrespect in the future. How can a boy or girl look with filial love and respect upon a parent who is debasing the God-given power with which he has been blest until he is as low or lower than the brute creation?

A father visited his son, who had been placed behind prison bars for a heinous crime committed while drunk. The son turned upon the father with a curse for the pernicious example that placed him in a criminal's cell. A young man about to be hung was approached by his mother. He thrust her aside with an oath, saying: "You are no true mother. Had you done your duty I had never been here." These are not isolated cases; there are many such. Pause and think a moment and you may count by the dozen parents, even in this town, who fail to instil into the minds of their children correct principles—principles calculated to make them upright, honorable members of society. You will find many such among those whose names are on church books and who are deeply, vitally interested in the heathen world beyond the sea, utterly forgetful of the heathen in their own household. The work among the children of such parents must be done by the teacher if it be done at all. The ideal home and home influences would leave only supplemental work for the school room in this direction; but alas! there are few ideal homes, and many, very many, where the children, like Topsy, "just growed."

We may teach the children the effects of tobacco and alcohol in stunting the growth of the body. We must show its action upon the brain; how it first excites, then weakens, and finally deadens and destroys. We must show how the moral and spiritual sensibilities are blunted and at last lose all power of action. All this is the province, and thank God, in many states it has been made the duty of the various school teachers to do. But how shall it be done? Did you ever hear of the school master who had a good boy's book, filled with pleasant stories, attractive pictures and beautiful gems of art? When a boy had been specially good and studious, he was permitted to turn the pages of the charming book and peruse its contents for a time. This same school master had another book filled with the terrible accidents that had befallen disobedient, undutiful boys, and of the dreadful end that followed when they grew to man's estate.

The bad boy was placed upon a stool in a conspicuous place and required to devote a half-hour or more to the perusal of the bad boy's book. The good and the bad were thus placed before the boys, the good made pleasant and attractive; the bad painted in all its hideousness. You who know child-nature will understand how the boys delighted in the beautiful and abhored the other one.

It is recorded that this school master was able to rejoice in the fact that every boy entrusted to his care through a long period of years, became an upright, honorable man. Some such device as this would be excellent in teaching the advantages of a temperate, well-spent life, and the horrors and disgrace of one devoted to intemperance.

As it is better to lead a soul to Christ by pointing out the beauties of the Christ character in his love and mercy toward fallen man, rather than by forcing him into the kingdom because of the terrors of divine wrath, so it is better to lead our boys and girls to choose sober, industrious, God-fearing lives because of the beauty in such characters rather than by holding up to them constantly the dreadful consequences of indulging in sinful appetites and habits.

You look at a beautiful picture. The soul is instinctively elevated. Higher, loftier aspirations fill the heart. You are better from that hour. Again you look at a picture wherein is depicted crime and its punishment. You shudder and turn away, and from that hour because of fear that the same punishment may come to you, you abstain from that form of sin. In the first case your whole being is elevated. You are a better man or woman. In the second, you simply give up something because you must, and while you escape the consequences you dread, you are not made so very much better thereby.

Let the teacher paint word pictures of what a noble, manly boy may become. It is sometime needful to point out the end of the disobedient and vicious, but it is most unwise to make this the prime motive prompting our boys and girls to lead pure, true lives. And yet is it not true that this is the very thing we do? Parents, you too have a valuable lesson here. When your boy or girl is tempted and falls by the way try the effect of earnest, loving entreaty. Give him or her a helping hand. Abstain from cruel, unkindly censure and your children will rise up and call you blessed.

To be sure there are times when patient forbearing and entreaty cease to be virtues but such times are very rare. There are in the world comparatively few children in whom one is unable to discover elements of good. Find the good points, wisely direct, and a manly man is the result where otherwise there had been a drunken loafer.

Looking back over the twenty-five years in the schoolroom as a teacher of youth, and recalling the about four thousand boys and girls that I have enrolled as pupils for a longer or shorter period, I can count on the fingers of one hand all of those in whom I was unable to discover good points of character and who might not with suitable home and school training have developed into honored, useful members of society. While I may not say with the teacher just alluded to that not one of my pupils have turned out badly, I can say that so far as I was able I have tried to instil into the minds of my boys and girls, for I call them mine, principles of truth, justice and sobriety. Just what has been my success, eternity alone will reveal.

Let the parent and teacher work hand in hand in lifting up our boys and girls. Let suitable home influences surround the child, these supplemented by wise instruction in the schoolroom, and good results must follow.

But, my friends, permit me to say in conclusion, that while it is possible in this way to accomplish good work, yet it is my firm conviction that there is still one thing lacking—that thing, love and reverence for the Lord Jesus Christ in the child's heart.

250

MISCELLANY

We as teachers may aid in the development of the child up to a certain point. We may have to do with his moral nature so far as it relates to his becoming an upright, honorable citizen; here our work ends and it remains for your parents, for you, women of the W. C. T. U., for you, Sunday school teachers, for you, pastors and ministers of the gospel, to lead him out into the light and liberty of a child of God.

This done and he is forever free from the thralldom of sin and, so far as he is concerned, the drink power is relegated to the vile depths from which it sprung.

The Lord hasten the time when our boys and our girls shall thus fix their hearts and minds on God.

Then shall the desert rejoice and blossom as a rose. The mountains and the hills shall break forth into singing and all the trees of the field shall clapp their hands. Then instead of the thorn—intemperance—shall come up united homes, happy households, instead of the briar—drunkenness—shall come up the sweet incense of spirits freed forever from the shackles of sin, and these shall be the Lord for a name, for an everlasting sign that shall not be cut off.

OUR BOYS

(Walla Walla, 1897)

"To be a man were privilege," so the poet sings;

In form so like his Maker, and with a mind that brings

Him close to the Omniscient, hence we look with joy

Upon the brave, the earnest, the stalwart, vigorous boy.

We know the years must bring him to his high estate,

And we humbly ask that ever it may be his fate

To live pure and true, unspotted, with a consciousness within

Teaching him to walk the right way avoiding paths of sin.

Our boys—our hearts beat faster that we may call them ours,

And yet we tremble as we think that if their wondrous powers

Are developed as they ought to be, the parent, teacher, friend,

Must work in perfect unison that what they do may blend

In one harmonious pattern without a flaw or break,

So perfect in its symmetry that the whole may make,

When fashioned, with both care and thought according to God's plan

The noblest work in all the world—a truly manly man.

MISCELLANY

Our boys are like all other boys, their faults are not
    a few;
And yet they're active, brave and strong and in the
    main are true.
Bad habits, yes, but they will take the kindly admon-
    ition
When gently given and will show a truly deep con-
    trition.
'Tis ours to cultivate the lad with earnest wise en-
    deavor;
Nourish good traits uproot the bad, for they must
    live forever,
As we sow the seeds for them, so shall the harvest be.
Which they and we must reap at last in long Eternity.

OUR GIRLS

(Walla Walla, 1897)

'Tis a theme of great interest for what can replace
When once taken from us the sweet girls who grace
So many a hearth stone? what blessing and joy
They bring to our hearts! and yet an alloy
Very often creeps in to deaden the charm
Of their sweet girlish presence and quickly disarm
And trail in the dust their influence grand,
God-given, to bless the homes of our land.

Perhaps in no city all the world 'round
Can more beautiful or charming maidens be found
Than those who our homes and firesides adorn.
Yet sad to relate, one can in no wise conform
To the truth, and say, that unlike other places
Our girls have all added to beautiful faces
Sweet graceful manners, both winning and kind,
And that other great charm a richly stored mind.

MISCELLANY

It is certainly true as all must confess,
That they, in most cases, really possess
Much that's attractive, yet 'tis equally true
That some are possessed of faults not a few,
Grave sins and vices we quite often find,
Have tainted some heart, but if we'll not be unkind
Permit me to speak of follies less rare
That hold with firm grasp our girls young and fair.

With your permission, we'll go on the street,
And here we find girls both pretty and sweet,
But what in the world ails the dear creatures
That they so twist and distort their beautiful features?
One is led to exclaim: "Oh! can it be true
That they, like their brothers, are learning to chew?"
Alas! such is the case but the substance is black,
And is not called tobacco, but has another name—
    Jack.
We go to the church, to a lecture or ball,

The gum power has entered and holds in its thrall
Many girls we find there; and when they're addressed,
The language they use it must be confessed
Would not look well in print, unless you like slang,
Hear that girl naively say, "ar'nt you off your bang?"
We turn away in disgust and what do we hear?
But another exclaiming, "don't go off on your ear."

Thus the gum and the slang and powder on faces
Are stealing the power and destroying the graces
Of the ones dearly loved, the girls of our town—
The girls who on folly and sin ought to frown.
For to them in large measure the good Lord hath
    given
The power to lead souls to hell or to heaven;
Remember, dear girls, there's a crown to be won,
And the faithful will hear from the Master—"well
    done."

MISCELLANY

A TRIBUTE

(Walla Walla, 1897)

Tall, weird and grand, their vernal tops mirrored in
    the
Bosom of their lakes, the monarchs of the Coeur
    d'Alenes
As silent sentinels stand. Grim warriors dating
Back their ancestors to a time before the birth
Of man. The ages that have come and gone since then
Have only made them more sublime.

As sure and steadfast as the lofty hills that
Clustered 'round Jerusalem when sacred poets sang,
So stand these pine-clad mountain peaks, and here the
    sparkling
Waters of a lake find egress by a river
Broad whose crystal depths glisten in the sun, then
    move
Along to make the valley glad—the beautiful Spokane.

THE WIDE NORTHWEST

A wondrous picture in an emerald frame,
The valley lies as level as a floor, while all
Around Dame Nature in prodigal profusion
Has scattered gems of beauty. The rising sun ne'er
Looked upon a fairer scene. And here in other days
Before the white man came there dwelt two Indian
    tribes,
  The Spokane and the Coeur d'Alene.

Here they roamed at will, fished in the limpid streams
Or followed the swift-footed deer; here the mountains
Echoed with the dreadful whoop of war or smiled
In answering to the melody of peace.
Here in their rude simplicity they dwelt apart;
They lived and loved, then passed away to
The Red man's paradise.

MISCELLANY

No man can tell how long they lived thus, finding
Happiness or woe in their rude and barbarous way;
But some fifty years ago there came to them
A noble man who hungered for the Red man's soul
And who was willing to surrender home and friends
That he might lead these savage men to Calvary's
    cross.

This noble man was Cushing Eells, a man so like
The blessed Master that his very presence spoke
Of things divine. Eternal ages only can reveal
The good that he accomplished or the sacrifice
He made in path of what he deemed his duty.
Privation, danger, hardship, all were nothing
To this mighty man of God.

THE WIDE NORTHWEST

The red men speak of him today with reverence.
His is a fragrant memory, though dead, he lives
Again in the lives of many who were made
The better by his Godly life. But not alone
Was he the Indian's friend; there stands to-day a
Monument built by him in honor of a friend,

That friend the sainted Whitman whom all delight to
Honor so, that some times they forget the credit
Due to Father Eells. Be it mine to lay this
Little tribute of respect and love upon
The grave of him who needs no monument graven
By the hand of man.

It was my privilege as a pioneer
Of the great West to call this good man friend,
And many are the acts of kindness received,
From him. His life has even been to me a
Storehouse full of kindly acts and noble deeds
From which to draw at will the lessons that were
Needed oft to help me in discharge of duty.

The following lines were written for a Thanksgiving
entertainment held in the First Baptist Church at
Walla Walla in the fall of 1898.

TWO PICTURES

'Tis the good year Seventeen Ninety-eight;
The time, the glad Thanksgiving day,
The scene, a New England country home,
With farm house old and stained and gray.

From its ample doorway, one by one,
The aged parents have seen them go,
The boys and girls to make other homes,
And their hearts have bled that it must be so.

But now the harvest is garnered in,
The fruit is gathered, the nuts in store;
The boys and girls have come home again,
And their children troop through the open door.

THE WIDE NORTHWEST

There is joy around the family hearth,
The grandsire and the grandame gray.
Live over again the days of youth
As they watch the happy children play.

The table is loaded with wholesome fare;
There's turkey, the pies and the oyster stew;
A whole roast pig with corn in his mouth,
Doughnuts and apples and cranberries too.

In fact such a feast as our grandmothers knew
So well how to spread, and when grandsire's grace
Has seasoned the food, each guest in his place
Partakes of the viands content in his face.

MISCELLANY

'Tis a happy time for parents and friends
A day of reunion, a day of good cheer,
A day of thanksgiving when all recount
Their blessings and joys, best day of the year.

But a hundred years have come and gone,
The scene has changed to away out west,
In the land of the mighty Oregon,
And we visit another dear home nest.

This time it is not a family hearth
Where parents linger all the while
To greet the wandering boys and girls
And welcome them home with sunny smile.

But 't is a cozy church of God
Whose many members come to bring,
With grateful hearts an offering,
In the name of Christ, their blessed king.

The turkey and the roasted pig
On bill of fare we do KNOTT find
But STACKS of CABBAGES are there,
And LEMMONS of the choicest kind

There are JAYCOCK, also young and old,
And GRAHAMS of the choicest brand,
And ELY'S, not of the slippery kind,
For these thrive only on the land

Then there are dainties served in BOWLES,
I wot not but the BREWER knows
What caused the BURGESS of old time
To snugly fit his ample clothes.

In all a dainty bill of fare
And none need go off in a HUFF,
For surely with such ample spread
For every one there is enough.

And yet dame Kate who has a PAYNE
And several others loudly cry:
The dinner is not yet complete.
We need a HUCKLEBERRY pie.

THE WIDE NORTHWEST

Here the KIRKman comes with joy to dine,
The GARDNER lays his work aside,
And the COLEman comes with wife and child
While the pleasant KNIGHT is still a bride.

But I may not stop to name them all,
The HUNGATES and B. Y. P. U.,
Or boast of an abundant CROPP,
Or of Betheden girls so true.

It is enough to simply say,
That as the smiling faces blend,
They tell of Christ's love in the heart
And speak of joys that know no end.

MISCELLANY

It is a picture fair to see,
This gathering of fraternal clan
Ready to fight unitedly
For God and home as single man.

NOTE—The church had called as its pastor Rev. J. F. Huckleberry, who had not yet arrived.

The following lines were written for a club party at Republic in 1905:

THE NEW WOMAN

By L. L. WEST

I trust you'll not think me ungracious or bold,
If I talk on a subject which, "like apples of gold
In pictures of silver," has found a large place
In the "New Woman's" heart; with candor and grace,
She defends her position. It is progress you know;
The demands of the times would have it just so.

The old and effete, the new supersedes,
And the student of progress most wisely concedes
It is best. The "New Woman," the product of this,
The Century of Culture, should find her chief bliss,
Not in home ties and children; they are too common-
    place,
Life's horizon has broadened, the good of the race

Demands a surrender of these homely ties.
In this age of advancement must woman arise,
As Carrie Nation with hatchet, chopping off here and
    there
The boughs of obstruction, to let in the full glare
Of the rays of that Sun which some people call
"Social Equality" and Suffrage for all.

The "New Woman," ah me? a peculiar phrase,
I wonder sometimes is she worthy of praise;
Roman matrons of old had one chief desire,
In the hearts of their children high aims to inspire.
Our ancestors too were busy as bees
In rearing their children, and trying to please

The "Oaks of Creation" to whom they must cling
In loving dependence. Sweet incense we bring
To hallow their memory. But now what a change?
The shackles are loosed, and we must arrange
To accept new conditions, for woman you know
Is no longer a slave; for weal or for woe

Finds no place in marriage; divorces are cheap.
It is always much better to laugh than to weep.
The home is so tiresome, and woman's great need
Is easthetic Culture upon which to feed.
Then there's the "Aid" to take her attention,
And "Lodges" by far too many to mention.

MISCELLANY

The heathen afar, are in such great need
It is really enough to make her heart bleed;
And **fraternal** relations, how much in that word?
To neglect her dear Lodge were simply absurd.
Such stale duties as home and as children, ah me?
The "New Woman" in these no beauties can see,

Again there's the Club, the newest new fad.
Its joys are sufficient to make her heart glad.
Roosevelt surely did not know of these joys,
Or he'd never suggest, "It is she who employs
Her time and her heart in rearing the youth
Who is laying up treasurers of riches and truth."

THE WIDE NORTHWEST

A strenuous life should not touch the dear dame
Except as she labors for culture and fame.
Like "Topsy" her children must really "just grow";
'Tis enough that their mother of the Heathen should
    know;
Their own little foibles, their simplest needs
Cannot interest her. Let them grow up like weeds.

Is the picture o'er drawn? I hear you say, "yes."
An yet I am sure that you must confess
There is much of it true. Alas! we do find
Many mothers who ought to be tender and kind,
Who see in their home life but little to charm,
And naught in their children to occasion alarm.

MISCELLANY

The "New Woman," I am sure will be soon out of
    date.
She's a fad and must hasten to meet the same fate
That comes to all fads; then the woman of old
Once more resplendent shall shine as pure gold.
The dross cast away, the mother and wife
Shall be counted by all the best thing in life.

———

A holiday greeting sent to old pupils and friends
after my seventieth birthday.

GREETING

Three score and ten,—pray call me not old,
Nor smile when I say, for I tell you in truth,
As the years pass away and new years unfold,
I drink from the fount of perennial youth.

Gray hairs may have come, and wrinkles a few,
Still the heart is unchanged and active the brain;
Though endurance is less, it really is true
My thoughts running riot are hard to restrain.

But they must be curbed, while I bring you good cheer;
A message of love and fellowship sweet;
Thus putting real meaning in the "Happy New Year,"
Which as garland of roses, I lay at your feet.

THREE VIEWS OF LIFE

The pessimist tell us the world is awry,
Not a single good thing in earth, air or sky;
All human life is made up of sorrow
He catches no glimpse of a happy tomorrow.
With a sigh and a groan and a look of despair,
He is sure there is really no good anywhere;
The world gone to pot, and to certain disaster
Is full of great evils nobody can master.

His doleful song sung, with a satisfied smirk,
He calmly awaits the results of his work;
For the seeds of unrest which he has been sowing
Must grow harvest of grain not worth the mowing.
Opposed to this croaker, the optimist smiling,
Comes singing his song, bewitching, beguiling
Till you come to believe all wrongs have been righted
And the other poor fellow was really benighted.

But here comes another who, after surveying
Existing conditions, is cheerfully saying;
"While some things are bad, I really have found
Much to commend as I looked around.
Evils there are which surely need righting,
But they give us courage and real zest for fighting,
It is up to us fellows to sound the alarm.
Then go forth and wipe out the things which do harm.

MISCELLANY

FIFTIETH ANNIVERSARY OF THE
FOUNDING OF COLFAX

Several years ago when Colfax had planned to celebrate its fiftieth anniversary, Hon. Jas. A. Perkins, generally recognized as the father of the city, died just prior to the date set. The committee in charge invited me to speak in his stead. I said in part:

There is in every normal human heart a desire for change; a wish to delve into the unexplored, or unknown. It was this call that prompted the denizens of the Mississippi valley, and other sections of our country to cross the "Great Divide" and to come over and possess the "land of promise." The "You must show me" Missourians, the Hawkeyes, the Badgers, the Hoosiers, the Wolverines, the Suckers and many others from all sections of our great United States gave of their brightest and best to make up the population of our magnificent domain, soon to be celebrated in history and song as the great Palouse country.

We were a cosmopolitan people; socially, politically, religiously, professionally. We represented all classes and grades of human society; we represented also a remarkably high grade of intelligence, much higher than the average in pioneer communities and the beautiful feature of our population was that we were able to amalgamate into one great, integral whole. There were no casts; no one, from a social standpoint, higher or better than his fellows.

THE WIDE NORTHWEST

The Colfax of 1875 to 1880, representing in its population so many different classes and conditions was surprisingly free from the petty jealousies and the frictions which mark the social life of so many of our modern communities. We were an aggressive and a progressive people; aggressive in the sense that we must take virgin territory and hew out for ourselves a destiny; progressive in that we must build not only for ourselves but for future generations. It was "up to us" to lay the foundations for that development that should make the Inland Empire rejoice and "blossom as the rose." It is for you to judge how well we succeeded in our mission. We were an hospitable people, the latch string was always out, our homes and tables were shared by the strangers within our gates to an extent seldom seen in these days of frenzied business and high finance when every man is for himself and practically against every other man.

We were a social people, delighting in innocent pleasures and social intercourse which make life worth while; and let me whisper in your ears we did not always have to resort to the dance or the card party for public amusement.

We were not as religious a people as we should have been and yet we laid the foundations for the magnificent edifices that are now the homes of our various denominations. Witness in proof of this the beautiful churches which adorn your streets here in Colfax.

We were a people interested in the education of our

youth, and Whitman county ought to be proud of the fact that to her and to Colfax, her county seat, belongs the honor of establishing and maintaining for a period of years the first high school in the Inland Empire and, with the exception of the Territorial University at Seattle—then a very small school—Whitman Seminary and St. Paul's School for Girls in Walla Walla, the only high school in the territory of Washington.

It is proper that I should mention a few of those who stood out prominently among our pioneers. The first of these, of course, is Honorable James A. Perkins. Some others who ought to be mentioned in this connection are Captain James Ewart, his wife, John C. Davenport, Hez. Hollingsworth, Len Reynolds, James Taylor and others.

I desire to call attention to the fact that the whole Inland Empire is greatly indebted to Colfax and to Whitman county for the material prosperity which has made so many of these communities the prosperous, populous places that they are today. This is notably true of Spokane. Much of the material wealth and many of Spokane's most aggressive citizens laid the foundation for their money and success in life in Whitman county. I have only to mention Hon. Jacob Hoover, the founder of what is known as the Spokane Eastern Trust Company; E. T. Coman, president of the Exchange National Bank; Aaron Kuhn, C. B. King, the veteran stage man; Thomas Brewer of the Fidelity Bank and many others. What was true of the people going into the banking business is equally true along other lines of human endeavor; lawyers, doctors, teachers, professional men of all lines received much of their early training in Whitman county. I shall not take your time to mention the names of these, but if you will take the trouble to take the Spokane directory and go through it you will find that many of the retired business men and capitalists of Spokane owe their prosperity to the golden grain raised in Whitman County and I will venture the assertion that a very large number of the automobiles owned by their possessors in Spokane and vicinity were purchased and paid for with "Whitman county money."

In closing I dedicated the following lines composed in 1897 to my friend of the olden time, of whom there were none truer, James A. Perkins.

FRIENDSHIP

The sweetest thing in human life is friendship,
The golden cord binding two hearts together
E'en as David's soul was bound to Jonathan's.
Coming to bless and cheer the race, it takes strong
Hold upon the Infinite. It reaches out to that
Within the vale and speaks a heavenly language.

Heart speaks to heart in calm and sweet communion;
It hides no faults, but patiently endeavors
To foster good traits, uproot the bad and make
A character such as God can own and bless.
Deep and quiet as a mighty stream, it runs
Its silent course and joins the sea—Eternity.

As some unruffled lake, whose placid bosom lies
Basking in the summer's sun, thus finding peace
And warmth, so is friendship, calm and still, unlike
That other passion we call love, which has its
Heights of bliss and depths of deepest woe, and is
As full of whims as any child that's spoiled.

Blessed be friendship, he who has a friend in
Truth should count himself more fortunate than he
Whose wealth is told in millions; and yet how few
There are who at all appreciate the worth of friends;
But rather seek to make pleasant path in life
By falsehood and abominable deception.

To truly have a friend one must himself be
Truly friendly; must accept the stings that
Come from friendly criticism in a way that shows
His heart is ready to accept the truth and
Profit by it. Then will true friendship bring
Peace and comfort to the weary soul of man.

A PRAYER

As I sit alone in the gloaming
And ponder of days gone by,
Of days that brought joy and sorrow,
Of days that are gone for aye.

My heart is sad for the errors
That here and there I see,
And I pray the Heavenly Father
That my life henceforth may be

The life of a faithful servant;
A follower of that One
Who guides and helps his children,
And rewards when life is done.

And I pray that he will always,
With tenderness and love,
Direct my faltering footsteps
In the way that leads above.

With Him to guide, the present,
So full of hopes and fears—
So full of joys and sorrows,
Of heart-breaking sighs and tears,

THE WIDE NORTHWEST

Is robbed of all that is painful
And filled with blessings rare,
While the future is full of promise
And freed from worrying care.

With this prayer for help and guidance,
I find that I grow strong
To do each day my duty
And to overcome the wrong.

July, 1885.

BEAUTIFUL DAISIES

Under the sod where the daisies bloom,
  The beautiful, beautiful daisies,
Our fathers are sleeping within the tomb,
  They hear not our sighs or praises,
They are quietly resting, their work well done
  Awaiting the crown they so nobly won.

Our fathers in blue—quick to heed the call,
  In the hour of need they marched away,
Surrendering home and friends and all,
  Ready for battle's stern array;
And now as we sing pæans of praises,
  They quietly rest 'neath beautiful daisies.

MISCELLANY

The years have come and the years have gone
  Since freedom's battle for us they fought,
And put down forever the giant wrong
  Of human slaves; with blood they bought
The priceless boon; and now their praises
  Are sung each year by beautiful daisies.

The sons of heroes now hear the call
  Of suffering Cuba and forth they go
To free their brothers from Spanish thrall.
  In their veins the blood of martyrs flow,
With deeds they will sing their father's praises
  Who sleep beneath the beautiful daisies.

We weep for our boys on the gallant Maine,
  But joy in the work at Manila Bay.
'Tis the hand of God against cruel Spain,
  Her power is lessening every day.
Soon we'll welcome our boys with joyful praises
  And weave for them crowns of beautiful daisies.

Just at close of the Spanish American
War and printed in the Walla Walla Daily
under direction of the women of the town.

I want to express my very great appreciation of the kindness of Mr. George W. Dodds, W. W. Hindley and others of The Spokesman-Review. To the management of the Chronicle, and all friends who have made it possible for me to publish this history of my life and work in the great State of Washington. Permit me to close with this bit which I wrote five years ago.

SCATTER SUNSHINE

Just scatter sunshine here and there,
As through this life you go
Remember sad hearts everywhere
Are bowed with human woe.

The happiness that you can give
Will surely bring great pleasure;
In joy of others you thus live,
And find life's sweetest treasure.

It is he who seeks to help his kind
Who finds true joy in living.
He emulates the Master mind
But gets while he is giving.